Anne Bradstreet

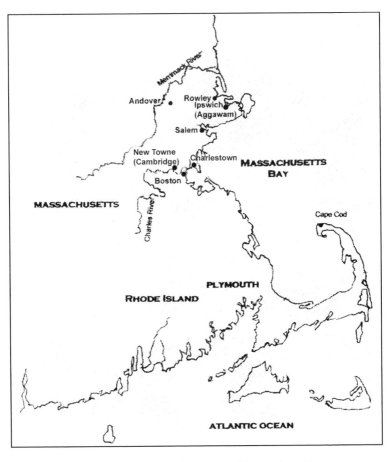

Massachusetts Bay in the days of the early settlers

Anne Bradstreet

Pilgrim and poet

Faith Cook

 BOOKS

EP Books
Faverdale North, Darlington, DL3 0PH, England
e-mail: sales@epbooks.org
web: www.epbooks.org

EP Books USA
P. O. Box 614, Carlisle, PA 17013, USA
e-mail: usasales@epbooks.org
web: www.epbooks.us

First published 2010

British Library Cataloguing in Publication Data available

ISBN 13 978 085234 714 0   ISBN 0 85234 714 6

Printed and bound in the USA

Strangers and pilgrims here below,
this earth, we know, is not our place;
but hasten through the vale of woe,
and, restless to behold thy face,
swift to our heavenly country move,
our everlasting home above.

(Charles Wesley)

Contents

	Page
List of illustrations	8
Preface and acknowledgements	9
1. Formative years	11
2. The Great Migration	20
3. New world … new manners	29
4. When pilgrims disagree	37
5. From New Towne to Aggawam	45
6. The secret poet of Aggawam	53
7. New England woman	67
8. The two dialogues	75
9. Into the unknown	88
10. 'My rambling brat'	97
11. Strength in weakness	109
12. Eight chicks in a nest	118
13. Gathering clouds	130
14. A house on high	139
15. Seeking a better country	150
Appendix — Anne Bradstreet's biographical account left for her family	163
Notes	169
Suggestions for further reading	170
Index	171

Illustrations

Map of Massachusetts Bay · Frontispiece

James I · 12

John Cotton · 14

St Botolph's Church, Boston · 15

Initial letter of the Massachusetts Bay Colony charter · 22

John Winthrop · 25

The *Arbella* · 26

John Endecott · 29

Anne Hutchinson preaches to settlers · 40

Henry Vane · 41

Roger Williams · 43

Typical frontier homes · 48

A typical New England fireplace · 54

Anne Bradstreet writing · 59

Simon Bradstreet · 68

Charles I · 80

View of Harvard in the early days · 91

Title page of *The Simple Cobbler of Aggawam* · 102

Title page of *The Tenth Muse* · 105

Thomas Dudley · 111

Charter for the founding of Harvard College · 112

Stained-glass window depicting Anne Bradstreet · 120

Anne Bradstreet's signature · 125

Charles II · 131

Letter in Anne Bradstreet's handwriting · 143, 144

Part of the kitchen in a typical home of the period · 146

The new house built after the fire · 151

Title-page of the second edition of Anne's poems · 160

Preface and acknowledgements

An unexpected letter arrived on our doormat some months ago. It bore an American postmark and the name of my correspondent was unfamiliar to me, although a quick search of the Internet suggested that my ignorance was inexcusable. This friend had a suggestion to make: 'Why not write a book entitled *The Three Annes*?' The idea intrigued me, but as I thought about it, I realized that two of the 'Annes' (Anne Steele and Anne Dutton) had recently been covered in evangelical literature. But who was the third Anne, 'Anne Bradstreet'? Again, I soon discovered that my lack of knowledge was culpable.

The more I thought about Anne Bradstreet, the more fascinating her story became. Sailing to the New World in 1630 at the age of eighteen, Anne was among that first contingent of Puritan refugees leaving English shores between 1630 and 1642, an exodus known as 'The Great Migration'. Her upbringing ill-prepared her for the circumstances she met: hunger, privations and death on every hand. Overcoming her early problems, together with cultural obstacles which discouraged women from venturing into academic realms, Anne Bradstreet secretly composed reams of verse. Printed in England without her knowledge or permission, her work brought her unexpected and astonishing fame as she became America's first published poet — one whose works are still in print today. More than this, Anne's spirituality, her dependence on God in prayer, her constant desire to live as a pilgrim, evaluating her all — house, family, achievements — in the light of that better world to come, is a challenge to our frequently materialistic, earthbound outlook.

A recent flurry of interest has brought Anne Bradstreet's life and work to public attention in the last forty years. Several accounts of her life have been written, and I have found one by Charlotte Gordon, published in 2006, most useful. However, this is written from a secular viewpoint, and as little biographical material exists outside of Bradstreet's own writings, the work includes a considerable amount of fiction. P & R Publishing have also produced an attractive book by Heidi Nichols, with selections of Anne's poetry, but this mainly concerns itself with historical and literary aspects of her work.

First I would wish to thank Dr Curt Daniel, at whose suggestion I embarked on this work. I am also grateful to the artist LaDonna Warrick for her fine imaginative portrayal of the poet used throughout. Once again, the support, encouragement and help of my husband Paul have been invaluable, and our friend Ralph Ireland misses nothing as he searches my writing for mistakes large or small. I owe to both a real debt of gratitude.

May Anne Bradstreet's life encourage us to keep her perspectives in mind:

Here's neither honour, wealth, nor safety;
Only above is found all with security.

Faith Cook

1.

Formative years

King James I of England was angry. His patience finally snapped when he received yet another delegation of Puritan preachers urging him to grant greater religious toleration to men of their persuasion and to make further reformations in the English state church. The king had already been confronted by these issues on several previous occasions following his accession to the throne of Elizabeth I in 1603. Now he had had enough. Pressed once more on the subject at a conference convened at Hampton Court Palace early in 1604, he could only snarl contemptuously, 'If this is all your party have to say, I will *make* them conform or I will harry them out of this land ... or worse.'

Such ugly threats were not immediately fulfilled, but fulfilled they certainly were before the end of the reign of this king, known as 'the wisest fool in Christendom'. Some of the noblest and best citizens in the land were to feel the lash of his drive towards total conformity of religion and eventually be 'harried' out of the country.

James I (1566–1625)

Eight years later — years when religious intolerance was steadily increasing — a daughter was born to a Puritan couple, Thomas and Dorothy Dudley, a child they named Anne. Thomas Dudley, born in 1576, had been orphaned at a young age and had subsequently come under the influence of wealthy Puritan patrons. Early converted to God, he soon demonstrated an earnest and inflexible zeal for spiritual truth, laying down firm biblical guidelines for his life. Moving to Northampton, he entered the service of the Earl of Northampton as manager of his extensive estates. Before long Thomas married Dorothy Yorke, a wealthy and well-connected young woman.

Their first child, Samuel, was born in 1608, followed by Anne in 1612; then three more daughters, Patience, Sarah and Mercy, were added to the family during the next few years. Living in their own cottage on the Earl of Northampton's estate, the children had enjoyed a pampered and privileged childhood. But all was suddenly to change in 1620, when Anne was eight. Thomas Dudley announced that the family would be moving from Northampton to Sempringham, Lincolnshire, where he had obtained a fresh appointment, this time to act as steward to Theophilus, Earl of Lincoln.

Theophilus had inherited the title when he was only twenty, following the early death of his father, but with it he also inherited the burden of the family finances, which were in a chaotic state. With strong Puritan persuasions himself, Theophilus urgently needed a like-minded, capable and trustworthy steward to sort out his affairs and help to balance the books. Thomas Dudley came to his notice. An astute businessman, Dudley seemed the right choice for the task, and so it proved as he set about transforming the earl's interests.

The rambling Lincolnshire estate to which the Dudley family was introduced was a contrast to life in Northampton. The household was lively and active, for Theophilus had eight siblings all still at home, cared for by a retinue of fifty or more servants. The dowager Countess Elizabeth, the earl's hawk-eyed mother, a woman of staunch evangelical principles, was clearly in charge, supervising the whole family.

For eight-year-old Anne Dudley, an intelligent and studious child, the greatest pleasure of her new home was the books. The Earl of Lincoln's library was crammed with volumes — history, literature and religious writings — and it would seem that Anne had liberty to read to her heart's content. Added to this she had the privilege of sharing in the tuition provided for the earl's five younger sisters, some of whom were little older than Anne herself. The countess was advanced in her thinking for the times and strongly believed in educational opportunities for girls, a circumstance which held benefits that would influence Anne's entire life.

But of even greater benefit for Anne was the nearness of the new family home to Boston, and therefore to the

John Cotton

ministry of the great Puritan preacher John Cotton at St Botolph's Church. Each Saturday afternoon covered wagons stood ready to carry the family the fifteen miles that lay between Sempringham and Boston. The three-hour drive along muddy lanes through the low-lying Fen Country brought them at last into the bustling market town of Boston and to the Earl of Lincoln's Boston home. Here they spent two nights enabling them to join in worship with the congregation at St Botolph's.

John Cotton's searching ministry left a permanent mark on Anne, for she was a serious child. From an early age she had been troubled by her sins and often could not sleep at night until she had confessed them to God in prayer and felt his forgiveness. Writing many years later she records:

> *In my young years, about 6 or 7 as I take it, I began to make conscience of my ways, and what I knew was sinful, as lying, disobedience to parents etc. I avoided it. If at any time I was overtaken with the like evils, it was a great trouble, and I could not rest until by prayer I had confessed it unto God.*

Clearly Anne had been carefully taught God's moral law both by John Cotton and also by her mother Dorothy, whom she would describe as 'a true instructor of her

St Botolph's Church, Boston, England

family'. Although little is known of this self-effacing woman, Anne's later words point her out as a good mother, a woman of quiet godliness, who must have encouraged her children to read the Bible regularly at an early age. Anne herself found 'much comfort in reading the

Scriptures', but in common with small children everywhere she could as easily forget, or find herself not bothered to read or pray. Then with pangs of conscience she realized her neglect and redoubled her efforts.

The year 1620, when the Dudley family moved from Northampton to Lincolnshire, was one that would prove highly significant in Anne's life for another reason. For in September 1620, 102 men, women and children set sail aboard the *Mayflower* bound for the New World. Most were seeking religious freedom although some were emigrating largely for political or economic reasons. Fifty or more who sailed that month were English Separatists, known as such because of their desire to separate themselves from a compromised national church and form small independent gatherings of believers. Driven out at last by the intolerance and rigid demands of the Church of England — a fulfilment of the king's threat — they were seeking a land where they could worship God in peace. These Separatists endured a stormy sixty-six days at sea, often driven many miles off course. At last on 21 November the Pilgrim Fathers, as they later came to be known, cast anchor off the tip of Cape Cod, now Provincetown, Massachusetts.

But for young Anne Dudley these things were little more than an adventure tale; nor could the child begin to guess their relevance to her later life. For now her days were absorbed with the excitement of learning both from her highly literary father and from the lessons she enjoyed, together with those books she could read. Hers too were the trials of many childhood illnesses, far more serious in those days than now. In all these things God was working out his purposes for Anne. Probably at the age of nine or ten, she records 'a long fit of sickness which I had on my bed'. And in her convalescence, as the vacant hours slowly passed, the invalid began to think more deeply and to pray in a new and more urgent way. 'I often communed with my heart,' she tells us, 'and made my supplication to the Most High.' And God heard her prayers, for she added that he 'set me free from that affliction'.

In common with many young people, Anne admits that such periods of serious reflection proved only transitory, and she confesses that 'as I grew up to be about 14 or 15 I found my heart more carnal and sitting loose from God and the vanity and folly of youth take hold of me'. At such an age many high-born girls of this period would be contemplating marriage, and it may well be that Anne's 'vanity and folly' had some connection with twenty-year-old Simon Bradstreet, who had arrived at Sempringham several years earlier. Fresh from Emmanuel College, Cambridge, a college established thirty-six years earlier primarily for educating men of Puritan conviction, Simon was a man of strong spiritual commitment. He had been chosen by Thomas Dudley to be his aide and understudy in managing the Earl of Lincoln's affairs.

Although Anne was only ten when Simon first arrived, a friendship between the two clearly developed as Anne matured. His dark hair, dark eyes, quick mind and spiritual zeal fascinated young Anne. Biographers have wondered whether Simon's sudden removal from the Sempringham estate to serve the crotchety Duchess of Warwick had something to do with Anne's increasing affection for the young man, eight years her senior. This must be mere speculation. It is more probable that a fresh appointment was sought for Simon because at the age of fifteen Anne succumbed to the fearsome scourge of smallpox — a killer disease, particularly among younger people. Anne's life hung in the balance for some months and the removal of Simon may well have been for his own protection. The fear of the disfiguring pockmarks that often scarred a sufferer for life must have distressed Anne as she tossed backwards and forwards on her bed. Even if she survived, would anyone ever wish to marry a girl like that? But she could also see a divine hand behind her affliction. In her weakness and need she cried out to God for his mercy, this time not just for healing from illness, but for forgiveness of sin:

> *About 16 the Lord laid his hand sore upon me and smote me with the smallpox. When I was in my affliction I besought the Lord and confessed my pride and vanity, and he was entreated of me and again restored me.*

Even though she would accuse herself for not being grateful enough for her recovery, there is no doubt that Anne's experience of God's compassion and forgiveness was genuine and brought with it a renewed and spiritual mind. Her appearance was probably not severely marred by the pockmarks she had dreaded, for she makes no further reference to the condition.

More than this, she had the joy of Simon Bradstreet's return to Sempringham and in 1628, when she was still only sixteen, Anne married the twenty-four-year-old Simon. In a later tribute written by Anne to her husband, she describes the depths of their shared love:

If ever two were one, then surely we.
If ever man were loved by wife, then thee;
if ever wife was happy in a man,
compare with me, ye women, if you can.
I prize thy love more than whole mines of gold
or all the riches that the east doth hold.
My love is such that rivers cannot quench,
nor aught but love from thee give recompense.
Thy love is such I can no way repay,
the heavens reward thee manifold, I pray.

Even today these lines are considered to be among the tenderest and most beautiful of love poems in all literature.

2.

The Great Migration

As Anne, newly married to Simon Bradstreet, matured into young womanhood, the political and religious situation was becoming yet more fraught. In 1625 Charles I had succeeded his father James on the throne. Nor had the threats of persecution eased, for the new king's ritualistic and High Church tendencies were causing widespread dismay among all who were of Puritan persuasion. In addition he was demanding exorbitant loans from knights and landowners to fund his foreign wars.

The situation became acute in 1626 when none other than Theophilus himself, Earl of Lincoln, received an order to make the king a loan — one which he well knew would never be repaid. With his finances only just recovering under Dudley's careful management, Theophilus refused to pay so arbitrary a demand and as a result was thrown into a dungeon in the Tower of London to languish there until he was prepared to pay up.

The year 1628, in which Anne and Simon were married, would prove a critical one in the annals of English history.

In despair at the new king's taxation policies and his high-handed demands, Parliament presented him with a *Petition of Rights*, seeking just dealings between Crown and people both in taxation and social justice. But the effort proved abortive. More than this, the king appointed William Laud to the office of Bishop of London, a position which allowed this High Churchman to place men of Puritan and Separatist persuasions under even more pressure to conform. The Sempringham household became deeply perturbed. Where would all this end?

Only one answer seemed feasible. Like the *Mayflower* pilgrims of eight years earlier, they must flee the country and seek a peaceful future in the New World. Many were the consultations which took place between the Dudley family, the Bradstreets and the dowager countess Elizabeth, the driving force behind the Earl of Lincoln's family at Sempringham. And there was a further deciding factor. The dowager had a twenty-seven-year-old daughter, the Lady Arbella, whose strength of character, spiritual convictions and determination matched those of her mother. In her recent marriage to Isaac Johnson, a wealthy Puritan preacher, Lady Arbella had found one who shared her zeal and urgent desire to worship God in freedom. The couple were also in a financial position to undertake many of the preliminary costs involved in setting up arrangements for emigration to New England.

As tensions between Charles and his Parliament steadily rose, Isaac Johnson knew that the time had come for him to act. Gathering together a few influential Puritan leaders at Sempringham, including Thomas Dudley, Thomas Hooker, Roger Williams and John Winthrop, he was responsible for initiating the creation of the Massachusetts Bay Company;

Initial letter of the charter of
the Massachusetts Bay Colony

by 1629 the fledgling company had gained the king's permission, a royal charter, to settle a new English colony north of the Plymouth Bay settlement established by the Separatists nine years earlier. From the king's viewpoint this initiative might well rid him of some citizens whom he regarded as among the least compliant to his High Church agenda — men of Puritan persuasion.

The area to be colonized included a swathe of the New England coastland encompassing an area extending three miles north of the Merrimac River to three miles south of the Charles River, and as far to the west as it was then feasible to settle. Under the charter the new colony was to be self-governing, under a governor, an assistant governor and an elected body of eighteen 'freemen' (church members) who would meet four times annually to create laws and dispense justice.

The next step was for Isaac and Arbella to set up and finance a smaller preliminary expedition to prepare the way for a main emigration planned for the following year, 1630. With John Endecott, a man of steady and reliable judgement, appointed as first governor of the infant enterprise, together with a shipload of artisans, the advance party set off for the New World. Before long enticing reports filtered through telling of a land where fruit grew in abundance, where fish, fowl and other commodities were to be had in profusion. Food prices were high in England at the time but in this wonderland — so the hopeful emigrants learnt — strawberries, raspberries, plums and blueberries were all free for the picking; Indian corn grew abundantly, while cod, sturgeon and eels swarmed in the waters, with many lobsters 'great, fat and luscious'. Little wonder then that excitement ran high and an increasing number of families enlisted in the project.

Whether Anne was initially cheered by the prospect of a long and dangerous sea journey into the unknown and of never again seeing the gentle green meadows and woods of her homeland is unknown, but probably she was not. It was a demanding prospect for a young woman who was just married and still not eighteen years of age. A frantic year of preparation followed: a ship had to be chartered, provisions gathered, property sold, artisans in different trades encouraged to join the enterprise, household goods packed — the tasks were endless. But at last by Easter Monday in March 1630 all was ready. A large ship, once a frigate used to clear pirates from the high seas, had been commissioned and renamed the *Arbella* in honour of the young Lady Arbella.

150 feet in length, it could carry some three hundred passengers and a crew of fifty. Provisions for the long sea voyage and early settlement period had to be stored in the ship's hold: livestock such as chickens, pigs and sheep, ten thousand gallons of ale, salted meat and fish, together with oatmeal and flour, were all carried on board. Seven other ships were to sail in convoy with the *Arbella*, but in the event only the *Talbot*, the *Jewel* and the *Ambrose*, with their cargoes and passenger families, were ready to leave with the *Arbella*. The Great Migration, that large-scale exodus

from old England to New England which would take place over the next ten years, had begun with almost a thousand men, women and children in this first exodus.

Uprooted from home, country and friends, these Puritan families were made up of men and women set on pleasing God, seeking liberty to worship without the constant fear of persecution from state or church. To this end they had set their hopes on Massachusetts Bay as a place where they wanted to establish a system of government similar to that of Israel under the old covenant, a land where God reigned supreme in church and state alike. Perhaps they also hoped that by this endeavour the gospel of Christ would spread out far beyond English boundaries, even to the far places of the earth. But, like the patriarchs of old, they were ultimately seeking that better homeland — a heavenly one 'whose builder and maker is God'.

As the initial concourse of these would-be pilgrims gathered in Southampton waiting for the right weather conditions to prevail before embarking on their great venture, John Winthrop preached a memorable sermon, one known to posterity as the 'City on a hill' sermon although more correctly called 'A Model of Christian Charity'.[1]

Puritan leader, lawyer and a man of outstanding Christian character and devotion to the cause of God, Winthrop was now in his early forties. In 1629 he had made the decision to relinquish his title to Groton Manor in Suffolk and to sell up his estate. With the proceeds of almost £6,000 he contributed generously towards the fledgling endeavour and, like the Dudleys, Bradstreets and countless others, was prepared to sacrifice all the comforts of life for the sake of purity of worship and standards of godly conduct.

John Winthrop (1588–1649)

A tall, fine-looking man with natural leadership qualities, he was a clear choice for the position of governor of the Massachusetts Bay Colony. His words, therefore, in this sermon were packed with historical significance as a statement of intent for the venture. Not only should the emigrants aim at personal spiritual liberty and freedom to worship as they felt right, but this new colony must also be a testimony to all the world of the power of true religion and of the glory of God. Continuing his sermon, he declared:

> *We must consider that we shall be as a city upon a hill. The eyes of all people are upon us. So that if we shall deal falsely with our God in this work we have undertaken ... we shall be made a story and a byword throughout the world. We shall open the mouths of enemies to speak evil of the ways of God.*

With such noble resolutions resounding in her ears, along with a jumble of contrary emotions, Anne Bradstreet, her mother Dorothy Dudley, Lady Arbella and Anne's

The Arbella

younger sisters, Patience, Sarah and Mercy, now aged
fourteen, twelve and ten respectively, together with many
others, crossed the narrow plank leading onto the deck of
the *Arbella* and climbed gingerly down the ladders into the
women's quarters of the ship. As anchors were weighed
and the wind filled the sails of the heavily laden ship, the
Arbella moved slowly away from English shores. Many of
the women and children wept, as all the security they had
ever known gradually disappeared from view.

The crowded, squalid conditions of life below deck
would have been a severe culture shock to Anne and to
others brought up in genteel, even luxurious, circumstances. With hammocks slung closely side by side, all
privacy had now gone. Dank and dark with nauseating
smells, conditions were repugnant. Worse was soon to
come as a fierce storm arose which raged for three days
and nights. Tossed up and down by mountainous waves,
the apprehensive passengers on the *Arbella* feared that

their vessel would be battered to pieces. But all was well, and the travellers, though prostrated by seasickness, gave thanks to God for their deliverance.

Scarcely had the *Arbella* headed out of the English Channel into the Atlantic before it met a further danger: pirates! The coastal waters swarmed with these gangsters of the sea, and as eight unidentified vessels drew ever nearer the *Arbella* prepared for a fight. Women and children were hastily confined below deck, muskets trained on the approaching vessels, bedding deemed unnecessary thrown overboard; all was ready for an engagement — one against eight. Only as the suspicious ships drew within hailing distance did the apprehensive crew realize that these were not pirates at all, but English ships, bound for home, and posing no threat. Friendly greetings were exchanged in place of gunfire. The *Arbella* now had little to regret except the loss of valuable bedding.

Following these early incidents came three long and weary months as the *Arbella* made its uncertain way across the Atlantic. Fog, storms and the occasional sight of porpoises cavorting nearby broke the boredom of the interminable days. Sometimes debilitating illnesses eroded the hopes and anticipations of the travellers as a diet of salted meat, salted eggs, salted fish and bacon, supplemented by little more than dried bread and oatmeal, undermined their health. Scurvy became an ever-present threat, with one death on board. John Winthrop's journal describes his method for raising passenger morale:

Our children and others that were sick and lay groaning in the cabins we fetched out and having stretched a rope from steerage to mainmast we made

*them stand, some on one side and some on the other
and sway it up and down till they were warm.*

Such exercise improved circulation and helped to
bolster the spirits of adults and children alike. But perhaps
the arrival of a whale, blowing its fountain of water high
into the air, its enormous shiny back protruding from the
sea not a stone's throw away, was the most memorable
sight of that Atlantic crossing.

Towards the end of May came the news that they were
not far from their destination. Every eye was strained to
catch the first glimpse of their 'promised land' — the sweet
scent of vegetation, described by Winthrop in his journal as
'the smell of a garden', further raising their hopes. With all
the poetic sensitivity of her nature, despite her apprehensions, Anne Bradstreet must have felt a surge of excitement.

3.

New world ... new manners

At last on 12 June 1630 the *Arbella* limped into Salem Harbour, announcing its arrival with a blast of the ship's cannon. What had happened to the accompanying ships no one knew at the time, although all would eventually arrive

John Endecott

safely. Nor was there any encouraging welcome for the sea-weary passengers from those who had been sent in advance to prepare the way.

Desperate, half-starved and ill, the handful of men who had survived the bitter winter conditions of 1629 were hardly in a position to greet the newcomers. Their governor, John Endecott, had built a handsome home for himself, but most of that early party had only managed to erect inadequate wooden huts with damp mud floors; others had merely resorted to digging caves in the hillside. The filth everywhere was repellent.

Little wonder then that many years later Anne Bradstreet could still recall her horror at the situation facing her when the travellers disembarked. Recoiling at the discovery of such 'a new world and new manners', she admitted that her 'heart rose' against the conditions in which she found herself.

John Winthrop and Thomas Dudley quickly realized that Salem was unsuitable as a settlement and decided to sail further south. The whole region had recently been decimated by an epidemic of smallpox to which much of the Indian population had succumbed, so now the settlers discovered numerous clearings along the coast, abandoned and desolate.

Before long they arrived at a former Indian village, originally called Mishawaum, which had been taken over by a handful of the earlier settlers and renamed Charlestown. Perhaps, thought the new arrivals, this would be a suitable spot to set up their colony — that 'city on a hill' which these pilgrims so eagerly desired. There they erected a meeting house where they could worship together. They soon discovered, however, that their new home, situated on a narrow spit of land jutting out into the harbour north of the Charles River, was also inhospitable. Weakened by poor diet on the long outward voyage and unaccustomed to the blistering heat of summer coupled with the searing winds that buffeted the peninsula, the new arrivals began dying at a frightening rate. As Thomas Dudley would report, hardly a day passed without a further loss.

Then Anne was confronted with a death that touched her personally. Three months after their arrival Lady Arbella herself, Anne's friend from her childhood days and only about thirty years of age, sickened and died. And, as if this were not shock enough, Isaac Johnson, Arbella's husband, distraught with grief, died shortly afterwards. Two of the main leaders and inspirers of the party had been taken within a few weeks of each other. Things were at a low ebb.

John Winthrop knew he must take swift action to bolster their endeavour. In keeping with the high spiritual aims that had originally motivated these men and women, he arranged for all who were in sympathy with such aspirations to covenant together with vows of submission to one another and to God. They would promise to 'unite into one congregation ... under the Lord Jesus Christ our Head ... and bind ourselves to walk in all our ways according to the rule of the gospel...'

Anne Bradstreet, still only eighteen, was uncertain. She had found herself inwardly resentful against the horrors of her circumstances and distressed by the death and sickness all around. Why should she covenant together with others to join this new congregation? But if she did not, she would forfeit all the privileges of church membership, including her right to a share in communion services. Despite her misgivings, Anne knew inwardly that she must not rebel against God's purposes for her life, however distasteful they might seem at present. Overcoming her initial resentments Anne later wrote, 'After I was convinced it was the way of God, I submitted to it and joined the church.' Her name appears with others in that original covenant signed on 1 August 1630.

Increasingly aware that Charlestown was unsuitable as a settlement and determined to preserve their faltering undertaking at all costs, John Winthrop decided to move their primary location south of the Charles River to a more sheltered spot originally called Trimountain. Protected from the ferocity of the elements by the surrounding mountains and with a pure supply of water, the position seemed ideal. Calling this new settlement Boston, a name chosen to commemorate the ministry of John Cotton in Boston, England, John Winthrop relocated together with many other families. Carving out an area of land for himself of six hundred acres, commensurate with the amount of money he had invested in the project, he built a substantial home for his family.

Thomas Dudley, however, perhaps resenting Winthrop's dominant position, stubbornly refused to move from Charlestown, despite all the problems he and his family faced. So when a meeting house was opened in Boston, the Dudley contingent, which included Anne and Simon Bradstreet, was obliged to travel across the river each Sunday to join the congregation worshipping under the ministry of John Wilson, a friend of John Winthrop and a man of conscientious though rigid principles.

Although these early settlers experienced so many hardships and deprivations during their initial months in the New World, they had actually arrived in a part of the American continent that was abundantly rich in natural resources. A wide variety of crops could flourish there despite the wide swings of temperature. The small wild strawberries they discovered growing freely when they first arrived were indications that fruit of many varieties could be easily cultivated, including cranberries, gooseberries, grapes and later apples. Nuts of all sorts could be gathered in abundance, and big game such as deer and buffalo would supplement the meat supplied by pigs, cattle and sheep brought from England.

It was indeed a rich land, but Anne Bradstreet and her fellow settlers could scarcely comprehend this as the death toll in the infant colony mounted ever higher. By January 1631, just seven months after their arrival, Thomas Dudley recorded in his journal that at least two hundred had died and, although their numbers were partially replenished by further shiploads of refugees from Charles I's England, the outlook was bleak. Charlestown was clearly an unsatisfactory spot for a permanent settlement. Taking courage from the fact that the Separatist colony in Plymouth to their south, later known as the 'Pilgrim Fathers', had survived despite appalling early trials, Dudley realized he must lay aside his pride and move his family yet again.

Torn between the dangers of an exposed coastal position, with all the possibilities of attack from the sea, and the inland risk with the fear of assault from the Indians, Dudley, together with Anne's husband, Simon Bradstreet, chose the latter. Following the Charles River as it wound into the hinterland, they discovered a wooded area with twenty-five acres of meadows cleared by Indians some years earlier and now deserted. Here they could begin to build immediately and graze their cattle. Calling it New Towne, a name that would eventually be changed to Cambridge, the Dudleys and Bradstreets, together with a handful of other settlers, left the windswept, death-ridden settlement at Charlestown and began to build what they hoped might be a permanent home.

Not many months would pass in their new location before Anne herself was taken seriously ill. Given the alarming death toll among the colonists, she well knew that in all probability she would not recover. Just nineteen years old, she faced such an outcome with a detached stoicism. One of her early poems, written several years later, recalls her thoughts and fears at the time:

Twice ten years old not fully told
since nature gave me breath;
my race is run, my thread is spun,
lo, here is fatal death.

Life had seemed like a child's bubble, 'no sooner blown but dead and gone'. In the same way that she had submitted to her new circumstances in a strange country, Anne bowed herself under God's will with resignation:

All men must die, and so must I;
this cannot be revoked.
For Adam's sake this word God spake
when he so high provoked.
Yet live I shall, this life's but small,
in place of highest bliss,
where I shall have all I can crave,
no life is like to this.

Anne describes her illness as 'a lingering sickness like a consumption, together with lameness'. It may well be that in the low state to which semi-starvation had brought these hapless pilgrims, Anne had contracted tuberculosis, which had affected not only her lungs, but also her hips, bringing on a weakness in her legs which left her semi-lame for much of her life. Contrary to her fears, however, Anne did not die; she realized that God must have restored her life for his own purposes, even if these included correction and discipline. As she later wrote, this illness was sent 'to humble me and try me and do me good', and she hoped 'it was not altogether ineffectual'.

But Anne was also struggling with a private grief. Her love for Simon was intense and real. Yet why, after almost four years of marriage, was she still childless? Possibly not realizing that her emaciated condition and recent serious illness were likely to be contributory factors, she may have regarded this as a chastisement from God for her early critical attitudes to this 'new world', deprived as it was of all the comforts of her former life. Like Hannah in the Old Testament, Anne brought her distress to God in prayer, begging him to grant her a child. 'It pleased God to keep me a long time without a child,' she wrote, 'which was a great grief to me and cost me many prayers and tears before I obtained one.'

Anne had another secret, and one probably known to very few. In those long days before her prayer was abundantly answered with the arrival of her large family, her mind was turning back to an early interest — writing verse. The education she had enjoyed as a child had stored her mind with rich images and a heritage of classical history, together with a detailed knowledge of biblical history and the multi-coloured story of old England with its kings, queens and tyrants. Elizabethan poets such as Edmund Spenser, Sir Walter Raleigh and Sir Philip Sidney, whom the family claimed, rightly or wrongly, as their ancestor, fascinated her.

Above all the work of a French poet, Guillaume du Bartas, flooded back into her mind and became a model for

her own early attempts. Born in 1544, du Bartas came from
Huguenot stock and his epic poem *La Semaine du Création*,
translated from the French, was called *The Divine Weeks*. It
set out with high poetic skill God's acts on each of the
seven days of creation, becoming a prototype for John
Milton's great *Paradise Lost*. Anne was fulsome in her
praise of her favourite poet:

> *Thus Bartas' fame shall last while stars do stand,*
> *and whilst there's air or fire or sea or land.*
> *But lest mine ignorance should do thee wrong,*
> *to celebrate thy merits in my song,*
> *I'll leave my praise to those shall do thee right;*
> *good will, not skill, did cause me bring my mite.*

Should a woman really be writing poetry? Anne Bradstreet was not certain; nor were many others around her.
Undoubtedly this prompted her to keep some of her early
verse a closely guarded secret. For on everyone's mind at
that time was a situation that had arisen in the Massachusetts Bay Colony — a crisis which was tearing the infant
settlement apart. And the cause of the trouble lay at the
door of an erudite, gifted woman named Anne Hutchinson.

4.

When pilgrims disagree

The Anne Hutchinson saga had all begun back in old Boston, England, when this highly able and serious-minded Christian had been among the many who attended John Cotton's ministry at St Botolph's. Born in 1591, Anne Hutchinson was already a married woman of thirty with an ever-increasing family when the Dudleys had moved to Lincolnshire. Balanced and strong in her theological views, Hutchinson had followed Cotton's teaching, believing firmly that the justification of a sinner was the result of the unmerited grace of God, and did not depend on reaching a certain moral standard as a necessary prerequisite, or even entail a certain depth of conviction of sin. Verses like Romans 5:8, 'But God demonstrates his own love towards us in that while we were still sinners, Christ died for us,' were central to Cotton's teaching and therefore to Anne's thinking. The evidence that a regenerating work had taken place in an individual's life lay not in the attainment of an acceptable standard of conduct, good though that might be, but by the inner witness of the Spirit of God with the believer. The constant indwelling presence and guidance of the Holy Spirit was paramount in Anne Hutchinson's thought and experience.

In 1632, two years after his friends Dudley and Winthrop had left for Massachusetts, John Cotton's ministry was silenced by Bishop Laud's High Church demands. Cotton went into hiding at first, and then emigrated to the colony. Anne Hutchinson felt bereft of her pastor's guidance and in 1634 she and her husband, together with their numerous family, made that same dangerous journey across the Atlantic. They settled in Boston, Massachusetts, where John Cotton was now acting as pastor in the absence of John Wilson, who was temporarily back in England, seeking to urge his reluctant wife to join him. Once again under Cotton's ministry — a ministry that was being unusually owned by God, with 117 added to the membership during the year — Anne Hutchinson was content.

That same year John Winthrop's position as governor was becoming the subject of increasing criticism in the colony. So determined was he to keep Massachusetts as a pure religious state, untainted by any views he regarded as unorthodox, that he had become progressively more dictatorial, sometimes inflicting severe punishments for even minor deviations. Attempting to establish that 'city on the hill' to which all the world could look, Winthrop and other early leaders failed to see that by their demands for absolute conformity in all matters of faith they were perpetuating a degree of absolutism, followed by persecution, not dissimilar to the constraints imposed upon themselves in England, prior to their decision to flee. Had they not emigrated to escape the very same sort of thing?

In order to ensure such standards, Winthrop would rarely call the General Court to assemble or allow discussion on his decisions, even though the charter of the colony had stipulated that as governor he should do so four times a year. In what has been called 'the first political coup in the history of North America', representatives of the 'freemen' of the colony — male church members — gathered in 1634 to express their dissatisfaction with the present state of affairs. A system was then introduced which included two elected representatives from each settlement, or budding township, who would have powers to make laws, raise taxes and to re-elect the governor on a regular basis. Accordingly, Anne Bradstreet's father, Thomas Dudley, now deputy governor, was elected to succeed John Winthrop as governor of the colony.

Meanwhile Anne Hutchinson, a vibrant and strong personality, was gaining increasing influence. Adopting the important role of midwife to a number of young Massachusetts women, she earned the confidence and affection of many as she assisted them through the dangers of childbirth and supported them afterwards in care and friendship. But she made the mistake of thinking that in her adopted country she would have freedom to express all her deeply held beliefs, whereas in old England she had been obliged to suppress them. Gathering a few women together in her home, she began meetings for Bible study and discussion, basing her comments on Cotton's most recent ministry. Then things changed. John Wilson, the absent pastor of Boston, returned and took over the ministry once more. Anne Hutchinson was horrified at the contrast. Described as harsh and moralistic, Wilson preached largely on the demands of the law and little on the grace of God in the gospel. Anne judged him to be preaching a covenant of works and even to be unregenerate. She went further, noting similar traits in many of the New England pulpits. She even began to suggest that the only theologically 'sound' preachers in the Massachusetts Bay Colony were John Cotton and her own brother-in-law John Wheelwright.

Anne Hutchinson preaches to settlers gathered in her home

Anne Hutchinson became still more outspoken. Numbers attending her classes grew and before long influential men — artisans, merchants and magistrates — also began attending. For a woman to be teaching men would become an issue of major aggravation in the colony on scriptural grounds and one that led directly to clashes with the Massachusetts governors. Anne Hutchinson would soon discover that if John Winthrop had been hard on any who diverged from his strict standards of orthodoxy, Thomas Dudley was more so. Later he would be described by his own daughter, Anne Bradstreet, in an epitaph to his memory as:

To truth a shield, to right a wall,
to sectaries [any who deviated religiously] a whip and
maul.

Trouble was therefore brewing for Anne Hutchinson. The tension between legalism and antinomianism has always proved a complex one and has frequently destroyed the testimony of the unwary. Regarding all who disagreed with her as being under a covenant of works, Hutchinson, though orthodox before, gradually became more and more extreme in her views. Boldly and stubbornly she resisted the aspersions raining down on her from most colonist leaders. Only John Cotton stood by her. The accusation of denying the importance of the moral law of God in the life of a believer — antinomianism — was being firmly levelled at her.

But Anne Hutchinson was not without support. A sizeable contingent of colonists, particularly in Boston, supported her views. The arrival in New England in October 1635 of Henry Vane, a flamboyant but utterly sincere young nobleman, straight from the court of Charles I, was highly significant for the colony. He too had known a powerful work of the Spirit of God in his soul and well understood Mistress Hutchinson's position. Soon he would join

Henry Vane

her Bible discussion meetings, now held twice weekly with attendances of more than eighty. Dudley's initial period in office as governor was short-lived as Vane was elected to replace him in 1635. Vane's influence eased the pressure on Anne Hutchinson, but this increased again, especially when Vane's popularity waned as he made some early misjudgements. Before long Vane left Massachusetts entirely, and John Winthrop was re-elected as governor once more in 1637.

It fell to him to initiate proceedings against Anne Hutchinson, but when even her staunch supporter John Cotton turned against her, Anne's fate was sealed. The most serious indictment arose when she appeared to be claiming extra-scriptural revelations and personal and direct guidance from the indwelling Spirit. Winthrop's patience snapped. Pregnant with her fifteenth child, Anne Hutchinson was brought to trial by the General Court of Massachusetts in 1638 and found guilty of disrespect for the ministers. Called an 'American Jezebel', she was excommunicated and expelled from the colony. After a short period in the newly-founded town of Portsmouth, she eventually settled in Long Island, but her end was even sadder, as she and five of her children were murdered by Indians in 1643.

With such unbending attitudes towards any dissent in the colony, independence of thought was discouraged. The settlers in Massachusetts Bay had emigrated with idealistic dreams of a godly community where all sinful conduct could be held in check by severe penalties. But human nature proved the same on both sides of the Atlantic, and even draconian punishments failed to reform it. Old Testament laws were regarded as the norm by which misdemeanours were to be judged, particularly in regard to Sabbath-keeping. Whippings, stocks, mutilation and banishment were among sentences sometimes handed down for a variety of offences.

At the same time as the accusations against Anne Hutchinson were rumbling on, the case against an ordained minister, Roger Williams, flared up. A former friend of both Winthrop and Dudley, Williams had arrived in Massachusetts in 1631 with his wife and family, and for two short periods was appointed minister of the church in Salem. An erudite scholar and a

Roger Williams

man of deep spiritual conviction, Williams immediately began to show an unusual concern for the Indian peoples of the colony. He mastered one of their many tribal languages and, with true missionary spirit, felt that the colonists should seek to evangelize these people rather than supplying them with guns and other Western commodities. He protested strongly against the practice of annexing land from the Indian tribes without adequate payment, regarding it as sheer robbery and totally unchristian.

The real bone of contention, however, between Roger Williams and the leaders of the colony lay in his strong disagreement over the control exercised by the state over the church and over the individual conscience. The first

four commandments, those of idolatry, blasphemy and
Sabbath-breaking, were punishable by God alone and not
by the state, Williams insisted. With strong convictions on
religious liberty, Williams was the precursor of men such as
Oliver Cromwell and later John Bunyan and the Dissenters.
Although disagreeing with his old friend's contentions,
John Winthrop was distressed when Williams was put on
trial for his views in 1635. Refusing to recant, Williams was
banished from the colony. He had hoped to delay his
departure with his wife and family until the spring of 1636
when the harsh New England winter would have passed.
But, secretly warned by Winthrop of a plan being hatched
to arrest and force him onto a ship bound for England, a
solitary figure could be seen struggling manfully through
the thick snow as Roger Williams fled the colony. Eventually he would purchase land from the Narragansett Indians
and establish another settlement in Rhode Island which he
called Providence, in celebration of God's providential
dealings with him and with his family. Many who found
themselves unable to agree with the religious principles
governing Massachusetts found their way to Rhode Island
and here Williams is credited by some with founding the
earliest Baptist cause in America.

Anne Bradstreet would have followed all these unfolding events with mixed emotions. Even if she had secretly
sympathized with Williams or with Anne Hutchinson
(although there is no evidence that she did), she could not
be seen to disagree, as her own father was involved in all
the legal decisions concerning them. Her husband Simon
rarely took a different position from his father-in-law, so it
is not surprising that Anne has left little in her own writings to suggest her personal views on the crisis.

5.

From New Towne to Aggawam

With the benefit of better health and more settled conditions, Anne Bradstreet's prayers were at last answered and her longings realized when she became pregnant with her first child, probably late in 1633. Women frequently died in childbirth, for if complications arose medical help was limited and Anne knew well the risks she faced with a first baby. Her fears must have increased as her confinement drew nearer.

But all was well and, after six years of marriage, Simon and Anne celebrated the birth of a son whom they named Samuel, no doubt after that son for whom Hannah had once wept and prayed so urgently. And Samuel's birth heralded the start of their large and healthy family, as they would eventually have a further seven children — three more sons and four daughters.

Meanwhile life was gradually becoming more settled throughout Massachusetts Bay, with food supplies increasingly regular and housing conditions improving. New Towne, where Anne and Simon Bradstreet lived in a close-knit community together with the Dudley family and some sixty or more other settlers and their families, was even beginning to resemble old England in some ways. Anne loved to wander through the surrounding woodland and beside the meandering Charles River that flowed nearby. Lines such as these express her pleasure:

Under the cooling shadow of a stately elm
close sat I by a goodly river's side,
where gliding streams the rocks did overwhelm,
a lonely place, with pleasures dignified.
I once that loved the shady woods so well
now thought the rivers did the trees excel...

And always the beauty of the created world turned her mind to the glories of the Creator:

If so much excellence abide below,
how excellent is he that dwells on high,
whose power and beauty by his works we know?
Sure he is goodness, wisdom, glory, light...

But it was those very woods and trees which suffered most when a hurricane of fearsome proportions hit Massachusetts one August night in 1635. For three long days and nights its wanton damage wreaked devastation all over the young colony. Even the Indians said they had never experienced anything like it before. Trees were uprooted and tossed around like matchsticks with numbers of poorly built houses collapsing. The worst tragedies were in the bay itself, where ships were torn from their moorings and broken in pieces. Whole families perished as they were thrown into the turbulent waters. It is easy to imagine Anne's terror, now pregnant with her second child, as she lay in bed at night listening to the crashing of trees in those woods so near her home and wondered whether their own roof might disappear in the gale.

Perhaps it was the disruption of this event that caused Thomas Dudley to decide to move his family once more, this time away from New Towne. Room for expansion in the clearing was limited and each month brought more boatloads of immigrants fleeing the pressures of life in England. By now more than five thousand had fled Charles I's England and found homes in some twenty plantations or settlements scattered along the coast and some inland. In Dudley's mind it was time to enlarge the borders of their colony once more and conquer further virgin territory. Another possible motive for moving was to put a greater distance between himself and Governor John Winthrop. Sterner and more legalistic than Winthrop, Dudley always advocated a harsher line with 'offenders' such as Williams and Hutchinson, and New Towne was uncomfortably close to Boston. So now the entire family prepared to move.

Simon and Anne, with their toddler, Samuel, began to pack up once more. They were accompanied by Anne's older brother, also named Samuel, and his wife Mary, her younger sister Patience, married to a military man named Captain Denison, and her two unmarried sisters, Sarah and Mercy, now aged seventeen and fifteen. Their long trek north was bound for a semi-deserted coastal strip, originally called Aggawam by the Indians, but renamed Ipswich. Two days' journey lay ahead, much of it through uncharted territory, before the travellers reached the small frontier coastal town. Embarking on such a move with a young child at a time when she herself was advanced in

Typical frontier homes
Reproduced by courtesy of Maggie MacLean

her pregnancy was a demanding undertaking for Anne Bradstreet. It must have been a relief when they climbed the last hill overlooking the small settlement and saw the village stretched out before them. Sparsely populated though it was, it already had a small but well-established church, with its preacher, Nathaniel Ward, erudite but now ailing in health.

Some thirty families had built their homes in Ipswich, huddled together for mutual protection and comfort, for all were required to live within a half-mile radius of the small meeting house. Here and there were one or two somewhat grander structures where some of the wealthier and more influential immigrants had chosen to live — educated men who had brought their libraries with them. But close around the small settlement lay the dark, dense forests where dangers lurked, not so much from wild animals but from hostile Indian tribes. The Massachusetts Court had sent out warnings to Ipswich residents that each man must carry a gun whenever he ventured out, and a guard should be appointed to watch night and day and to warn of any approaching danger. The fears of a young mother like Anne Bradstreet in such circumstances can easily be imagined. She could only comfort herself by meditating on all that she had already known of God's protecting grace through a multitude of dangers. 'O Lord, let me never forget thy goodness, nor question thy faithfulness to me,' was her prayer, adding, 'Thou art my God. Thou hast said, and shall I not believe it?'

Initially Simon and Anne Bradstreet found themselves in cramped quarters together with many other family members while their new homes were being erected, but this may well have been a comfort to Anne as the birth of her second child was imminent. Soon after their arrival little Dorothy was born safely, probably early in 1636, and named after Anne's mother, as was so often the custom.

The crisis with regard to Anne Hutchinson was still coming to a head at the very time that Simon and Anne Bradstreet and Thomas Dudley, with his extended family, moved to Ipswich. Anne would have been acutely aware of the scorn being poured on a woman of intellectual ability, of vocal competence but of doubtful theology like Anne Hutchinson, and especially by her new pastor Nathaniel Ward, who had some scathing remarks to make about 'loose-tongued' females. How then could Anne hope to develop her own intellectual gifts and her strong desire to express herself in verse? It was not long, however, before she discovered that Ward, who was old enough to be her father and a known misogynist, also had a more tender side to his nature as he perceived in Anne a devotion of spirit coupled with an astute intelligence that appealed to him.

Ward had studied law and graduated from Emmanuel College, Cambridge, in 1603. He had travelled widely for the times, practising law both in England and on the Continent. However, his spiritual conversion during his thirties had changed the direction of his life as he entered the ministry. With circumstances changing in England and William Laud, Bishop of London, now at the helm in the church, trouble was soon brewing for Ward. But nothing could persuade him to compromise his stand for his principles and in 1633 he was deprived of his ministry. Although in his late fifties and a widower, Ward decided to sail for New England and settle in the far-off frontier village of Ipswich as colleague to a Thomas Parker, the first minister of the small church there.

Anne and her husband had not been long in Ipswich before Ward was obliged to resign his ministry on account of ill-health. However, he would remain in the settlement for a few more years, during which time he made his most important contribution to the establishment of a young America. As a skilled lawyer, Ward compiled a guidebook of official procedures for the colony called the *Body of Liberties*. Containing one hundred clauses, it protected personal property, safeguarded against cruel punishments, established trial by jury and made provision for the destitute. It concerned itself with taxes and citizens' rights, safeguarding the young community from many of the abuses perpetrated by Charles I on his people back in the home country. Deviating in some respects from John Winthrop's stance, Ward insisted that only those things expressly declared by Scripture to be 'morally sinful' should be legislated against by the state. Ward's work was adopted by the General Court of Massachusetts in 1641 and would eventually become part of the Massachusetts constitution.

The importance of Nathaniel Ward in Anne Bradstreet's life, and God's purposes in bringing her into contact with this prickly but lonely old man at an important time, would gradually become more and more apparent. Possessing an extensive library — a commodity that Anne much admired — and with a fatherly interest in Anne, he quickly realized that the young woman also had underlying spiritual problems which would undoubtedly draw out his pastoral concern.

In a frank admission towards the end of her life, Anne confessed her many doubts and fears during these days. 'Are the Scriptures really true?' she asked herself. 'How can I know there is a God?' Yes, she readily agreed, 'My reason would soon tell me by the wondrous works that I see, the vast frame of the heaven and the earth, the order of all things ...' that there is a God. But how could she know for certain that this deity was the triune God whom she worshipped and the Saviour upon whom she relied for redemption and eternal life? Realizing that such doubts were the direct assaults of Satan against her soul, Anne eventually fell back on a bare confidence that God had spoken in his Word and demonstrated the veracity of that Word many times over in her own soul.

Doubtless as her pastor Nathaniel Ward listened patiently to her fears and pointed her to the solid foundations of her faith, Anne regained some confidence. But then, Anne would ask herself, what about others who had fallen? In a veiled reference to Anne Hutchinson, she referred to 'some who have been accounted sincere Christians [but] have been carried away' by false teachings. This circumstance, she tells us, had made her cry, 'Is there faith upon the earth?' But even more than all the counsels of Ward, Christ himself brought consolation to Anne's troubled mind, until she could say, 'Return. O my soul, to thy rest; upon this rock Christ Jesus will I build my faith.'

6.

The secret poet of Aggawam

Life in a frontier village like Aggawam, or Ipswich as it was now called, was challenging, physically demanding and often frightening. Around each two-storeyed wooden home lay a large area of uncultivated ground, hard virgin soil, its size depending on the amount of capital each family had invested in the development of the new township.

For the Bradstreets this included space to develop a small plantation, grow sufficient crops for their ever-increasing family and make extra money as well. Part of the motivation in Simon's mind for moving from New Towne had been to provide him with sufficient land for such expansion.

Not only must Simon plant the wheat Anne needed to make into bread, but also vegetables of all kinds, and fruit where possible. Even apple trees could be set if he was able to obtain saplings from the homeland. In all probability the Bradstreets also kept an enclosure where poultry and pigs could be reared to provide meat for their young family and servants, especially through the bitter winter months. And,

A typical New England kitchen fireplace
Photo by Mary H. Northend (1850–1926), courtesy of Historic New
England/SPNEA

always, just beyond the newly established frontier village
lay the forest, silent, dark and threatening, its tall trees
outlined in black against the skyline.

A large central hall formed the most important room in
any frontier home of the time. Here the family cooked, ate,
entertained and even slept at times. A sizeable hearth
provided a focal point for all the family gatherings. Cooking implements, pots, pans and kettles were all ranged
around and hanging above the fireplace, where great logs
from trees felled in the forest were burning in the grate. A
smaller room lay at the back of the house, sometimes used
as a living room for servants or for storage, while there

would be two bedrooms, or a provision for more storage space, on the upper floor.

Simon, who had been appointed as secretary of the Massachusetts Bay Company and was therefore directly responsible to the governors, was often away on government business, and then the nights seemed long and lonely for Anne. With her children asleep, including the new baby, Sarah, born in 1638, all was silent apart from the occasional howling of wolves in the distant forest as they hunted their prey. And always there lurked the ever-present fear of attack from the Indians.

During those long, quiet evenings after the rest of her family were in bed, and far into the night, Anne would often sit gazing at the dying embers of the log fire that still glowed in the grate. Now and then a small flame would burst with a crackle and die. However, Anne's mind was far away. Lines of a poem were beginning to take shape in her mind. But it seemed useless. No one would ever accept that a mere woman could write acceptable verse. The spectre of Anne Hutchinson's disgrace rose before her eyes.

And, as if that were not enough to deter Anne Bradstreet from attempting to develop her poetic skills, there was the case of another intellectual woman, Anne Hopkins. This Anne too had attempted to write books, but, so it was rumoured, she had lost her reason as a result. Everyone knew that she had committed suicide by throwing herself down a well. The wise pundits around her asked whether this was because her brain was addled with too much learning. Even the godly and balanced John Winthrop had written:

If she had attended her household affairs and such
things as belong to women, and not gone out of her
way and calling to meddle in such things as are proper
for men whose minds are stronger, she had kept her
wits and might have improved them usefully and hon-
ourably in the place God had set her.

Yet, impelled onwards by her innate gift and the urge to
compose verse, Anne Bradstreet tried to push such
thoughts to the back of her mind. The poet in her was
demanding that she express the thoughts tumbling into her
mind in carefully chosen words, accurate metrical lines
and suitable rhyme. Perhaps she should speak to her
pastor Nathaniel Ward about her dilemma and share her
secret desire with him.

It must have been a surprise to Anne to discover that one
who was so well known for deprecating women as Ward,
and who had taken up a position hostile to Anne Hutchinson, would actually listen with sympathy to her aspirations,
see the merit of her early verse and encourage her to continue. We can picture the elderly pastor and the twenty-five-
year-old young mother wandering around Ward's extensive
library as he pulled out one book after another to show her.
Perhaps they would sit opposite the fire discussing some
aspect of classical or English history. On occasions he lent
Anne some treasured volume to take home to study at her
leisure. Anne soon discovered that Ward himself was
writing another book, not this time a legal work, but one
arising out of deep concern for the state of his mother
country, England, now teetering on the brink of civil war
between king and Parliament. Couching his material in a
sustained and quirky image of a cobbler mending boots,
'lamentably tattered, both in the upper leather' (the king)

'and sole' (Parliament), he would call his book, *The Simple Cobbler of Aggawam* — the Indian name for Ipswich. Perhaps at that moment Anne Bradstreet conceived the daring idea that one day she might become the poet of Aggawam; however, any such hope was little more than a distant dream.

Encouraged by Nathaniel Ward's support, Anne began to write. She had a strong desire to honour God and to serve his cause in the colony; perhaps she could even compensate in some way for the shame brought on womanhood by the failure of one such as Anne Hutchinson, whose disgrace hung like a dark cloud over their dream of a 'city on a hill', so dear to the founders of the colony.

Late into the night, with the darkness dispelled only by the unsteady light of a candle that flickered in the draughts, casting weird shadows around the room, Anne could be found working at the family table. Carefully, slowly, she began to fill numerous sheets of thin brown paper with her lines. She could not afford to make many mistakes, for paper was expensive and scarce. On and on she worked, her quill moving swiftly across her paper. Basing her style on that of her model and favourite poet of her early years, Guillaume du Bartas, she wrote verse that held an uncanny likeness to his as she began to explore similar grand themes, crammed with historical and classical references.

Poetic ability ran in the family and Anne's own father, Thomas Dudley, sometimes wrote verse. Not long before this he had composed an impressive work known as a quaternion, or a poem divided into four long sections. It was entitled *On the four parts of the world* and, under the image of four sisters, he described the contributions to civilization of Art, Music, Beauty and Wealth. Now lost, the work was apparently considered worthy of publication and Anne shared his pleasure when it appeared in print. In a poem dedicated to him, she expressed her satisfaction 'with the sight of your four sisters cloth'd in black and white'.

Anne therefore attempted something very similar — another four-part poem or quaternion, taking as her chosen theme the four elements: fire, air, earth and water. Personifying each, she depicted them as four quarrelling sisters, arguing between themselves as to which of them was the greatest:

> *The Fire, Air, Earth and Water did contest*
> *which was the strongest, noblest and the best,*
> *which was of greatest use and might'est force:*
> *in placid terms they thought now to discourse.*

Dispute as they might, each one claiming her pre-eminence over her sisters for almost five hundred somewhat tedious lines, they could reach no decisions. At last Anne Bradstreet put down her quill, surveyed her inconclusive lines, gathered up her long skirts and climbed the stairs to her bed — now long after midnight.

Without any satisfactory closure to the argument between the elements, Anne continues the dispute in a further long quaternion. Taking up where she left off, she begins:

> *The former four now ending their discourse*
> *ceasing to vaunt their good or threat their force,*
> *lo! other four step up, crave leave to show*
> *the native qualities that from them flow.*

Anne Bradstreet writing
Reproduced by courtesy of the artist, LaDonna Gulley Warrick

This second group of four she called 'The Four Humours in Man's Constitution' — the four basic temperament types: the sanguine, phlegmatic, choleric and melancholic. According to classical tradition, these were the eldest daughters of the four elements, so the choleric temperament was the daughter of fire, the sanguine of air, the melancholic of earth and the phlegmatic of water. In speeches lasting for another six hundred lines, the four temperaments hold forth on their distinctive virtues, but the arguments are more amicable than those of the four elements, with each being able to see merit in the other. And, in line with modern psychology, Anne concludes in the words of the phlegmatic temperament with the suggestion that few people can be easily classified under a single temperament type:

> Let's now be friends; it's time our spite were spent,
> lest we too late this rashness do repent;
> such premises will force a sad conclusion,
> unless we agree, all falls into confusion…
> Nor jars nor scoffs, let none hereafter see,
> but all admire our perfect amity;
> nor be discerned, here's water, earth, air, fire,
> but here's a compact body whole entire.
> This loving counsel pleased them all so well
> that Phlegm was judged for kindness to excel.

But Anne had not finished. Determining to write four such quaternions, she introduces us to 'the Four Ages of Man':

> Lo now four other act upon the stage,
> Childhood and Youth, the Manly and Old Age.

And these she describes as the firstborn sons of the four
temperaments: Childhood the son of the phlegmatic
temperament, Youth of the sanguine, Manhood of the
choleric and Old Age of the melancholic. In what is possibly the best of her quaternions, Anne weaves many
unusual and thought-provoking lines into her portrayal of
each stage of human life.

Childhood speaks first and Anne allows him a realistic
account of infancy:

> *With tears into the world I did arrive;*
> *my mother still did waste as I did thrive,*
> *who yet with love and all alacrity,*
> *spending, was willing to be spent for me.*

Childhood then confesses his ignorance and simplicity,
but also his sinfulness:

> *Stained from birth with Adam's sinful fact,*
> *thence I began to sin as soon as act:*
> *a perverse will, a love to what's forbid,*
> *a serpent's sting in pleasing face lay hid.*

Preserved though sickness, dangers and accidents, he
concludes:

> *I've done; unto my elders I give way,*
> *For 'tis but little that a child can say.*

Youth next takes the stage, boastful, impetuous and yet
realistic:

> *My goodly clothing and my beauteous skin*
> *declare some greater riches are within,*

but what is best I'll first present to view
and then the worst in a more ugly hue.

Young people would seem to have changed little over
the generations as Youth acknowledges sadly that he had:

My gifts abused, my education lost;
my woeful parents' longing hopes are crossed;
my wit evaporates in merriment:
my valour in some beastly quarrel's spent…
Sometimes I sit carousing others' health
until mine own be gone, my wit and wealth;
from pipe to pot, from pot to words and blows
for he that loveth wine wanteth no woes.

A bleak picture indeed of New England youth!

Nor is Anne too hopeful of Middle Age or Adulthood,
who is the next to speak. Certainly increased responsibilities have produced a degree of stability, but even the
satisfaction of cultivating the ground, of providing for
one's own, of fighting for the state can bring no lasting
joys, for:

… to conclude I may not tedious be,
man at his best estate is vanity.

Old Age then takes over and he has the most to say.
With a degree of realism he can look back over a lifetime of
stirring events. He recalls the days when England 'was
ruled by that celestial she', a reference to Elizabeth I. He
relives the horrors of the Gunpowder Plot, when Guy
Fawkes and his cronies tried to blow up Parliament:

I've seen from Rome an execrable thing,
a plot to blow up nobles and their king.

We can date this poem to mid-1642, for Anne refers to
the Civil War recently broken out in England:

I've seen a state unmoulded, rent in twain
But yet may live to see't made up again.

The years are creeping on, and a host of infirmities mark
Old Age's later days as death draws on apace:

My heart sometimes as fierce as lion bold
now trembling is, all fearful, sad and cold.
My golden bowl and silver cord e'er long
shall both be broke, by racking death so strong.

Yet Anne's own strong faith comes to the rescue, or else
the picture would be little else but gloom. As death calls
Old Age away, he can declare with assurance:

And I shall see with these same very eyes
my strong Redeemer coming in the skies.
Triumph I shall, o'er sin, o'er death, o'er hell,
and in that hope I bid you all farewell.

Almost as an afterthought Anne introduces one last set
of four, considerably shorter than the other three, compris-
ing a mere 260 lines, as opposed to several that are double
its length. Her final subject is 'The Four Seasons', but Anne
was tiring and her lines tend to be confused. In them old
England, New England, the signs of the Zodiac, Greek
mythology, Roman dating and biblical references all jostle
for a place. Fresh ideas seemed to escape her, and little

wonder, for she was pregnant with her fifth child at the time. Changing from her normal pentameters, or ten-syllable lines, to an eight-syllable beat, she concludes somewhat lamely:

My subject's bare, my brain is bad
or better lines you should have had:
the first fell in so naturally,
I knew not how to pass it by;
the last, though bad, I could not mend,
accept, therefore, of what is penned;
and all the faults that you shall spy
shall at your feet for pardon cry.

Four quaternions now lay on Anne Bradstreet's table, almost two thousand lines of rhyming couplets. Her achievement was little less than astonishing in view of her responsibilities. It had taken her almost four years to accomplish such a feat, for now it was well into 1642. Much of the time had been stolen from her sleep. Perhaps some had been composed while she was rocking her latest infant to sleep, for her family had been increasing steadily during these years. With Samuel, her eldest, aged eight, Dorothy and Sarah six and four respectively, and a second son, Simon, named after her own husband Simon, still only two, she was now expecting her fifth child.

But what could Anne do with such reams of verse? Who would dare to print a woman's efforts after the Mistress Hutchinson debacle? With no certainty of the quality of her work either, she decided that her best plan was to show it to her own father, who had encouraged her from her earliest days and whose knowledge of classical literature had stimulated her own. Two further poems were therefore

necessary before she could present her work to Thomas
Dudley: first a eulogy in his honour, and secondly a prologue introducing her lines. Somewhat obsequious in her
address, Anne presented her four quaternions as the
humble maidservants of her father's nobler verse, recently
published:

> *I bring my four times four, now meanly clad*
> *to do their homage unto yours, full glad.*

Realizing her debt to the poet du Bartas, Anne was
fearful that her father might think she had indulged in
plagiarism. No, she protested, her work was her own,
although admittedly influenced by du Bartas, of whom she
says:

> *I honour him, but dare not wear his wealth,*
> *my goods are true (though poor), I love no stealth;*
> *but if I did, I durst not send them you*
> *who must reward a thief, but with his due.*

Next she must write a prologue, and here she reveals
the most pressing problem she faced in her attempt to
compose verse — the contempt, even verbal abuse, heaped
on the head of a woman who showed signs of wishing to
excel in any intellectual attainment. 'I am obnoxious to
each carping tongue,' she complains. Clearly her neighbours had not been slow to criticize when they learnt that
Anne Bradstreet had strayed into a realm considered a
male prerogative. 'Who says my hand a needle better fits?'
she demanded. Worse than this, she found herself in a situation in which she faced defeat whatever happened. If her
work should prove acceptable, no one would believe it was

her own composition, or alternatively critics would maintain it was a mere fluke:

> *For such despite they cast on female wits:*
> *if what I do prove well, it won't advance,*
> *they'll say it's stolen, or else it was by chance.*

Even the ancient Greeks were more charitable, Anne complains. Were not the nine Muses, the Greek goddesses said to inspire both poetry and art, all women?

In case anyone should think that she, Anne Bradstreet, had exceeded her rightful place as a woman, she answers by pandering to male pride, yet still pleads for some small degree of credit for the attainments of her sex:

> *Let Greeks be Greeks, and women what they are,*
> *men have precedency and still excel,*
> *it is but vain unjustly to wage war;*
> *men can do best, and women know it well.*
> *Pre-eminence in all and each is yours,*
> *yet grant some small acknowledgement of ours.*

In the event both her father and her pastor Nathaniel Ward enthusiastically supported Anne's endeavours, enabling her to lift her head amongst her carping neighbours, impervious to their criticisms.

7.

New England woman

To imagine that Anne Bradstreet was little other than a secret poet, all her energies absorbed with the creation of verse and the care of her household, is far from the mark. An ever-increasing burden of domestic and social duties fell on Anne as her husband Simon was called upon to shoulder heavy responsibilities in the colony, and even more so when Dudley had appointed his son-in-law to undertake perhaps the hardest task of all — to oversee the creation of a union between all the burgeoning colonies in the New World. As immigrants continued to pour into the region from England during the decade 1630–1640, their settlements became ever more widespread. To amalgamate these disparate groups into a 'Union of Colonies', from New Haven to the Connecticut Valley, from Plymouth to Massachusetts, was no easy assignment and required all the diplomacy Simon Bradstreet was able to command.

Such responsibilities obliged Simon to be away from home for long weeks at a time, and Anne missed him sorely. Required to take on many civil and social duties in the absence of her husband, Anne would deputize for him on civic occasions; she must also attend to domestic matters, ordering sufficient seed for planting up their small-holding, settling disputes among those whom Simon employed, as well as advising younger women anxious over their children. Her

Simon Bradstreet

loneliness during Simon's many absences was intense, her love for him undiminished:

> *My head, my heart, mine eyes, my life, nay, more,*
> *my joy, my magazine of earthly store,*
> *if two be one, as surely thou and I,*
> *how stayest thou there whilst I at Ipswich lie?*

All she could do at times was to gaze at the faces of her children and see in them the 'true living pictures of their father's face'.

> *I weary grow the tedious day so long,*
> *but when thou northward to me shalt return…*

If only he would never leave her again:

... till nature's sad decree shall call thee hence:
flesh of thy flesh, bone of thy bone,
I here, thou there, yet both but one.

Simon's long absences negotiating a Union of Colonies among opinionated and often inflexible settlers kept him away from home for weeks at a time. This gave Anne many lonely hours and much time to think. As she cared for her family, nursed her children through various illnesses, anxiously hoped for rain for the crops during the blistering heat of summer days, or struggled to keep her family warm in the biting cold of a New England winter, she discovered numerous spiritual parallels to be learnt from each situation, and noted them down on scraps of paper. Perhaps one day she would gather them all together and give them to her children as a legacy by which to remember her. So Anne sagely comments:

> *If we had no winter, the spring would not be so pleasant: if we did not sometimes taste of adversity, prosperity would not be so welcome.*

From the varied trials she had faced and still encountered from day to day, she could write:

> *Corn, till it have passed through the mill and been ground to powder is not fit for bread. God so deals with his servants: he grinds them with grief and pain till they turn to dust and then they are fit manchet [a fine wheaten loaf] for his mansion.*

And, she added, still drawing directly on her own experience:

> *God has suitable comforts and supports for his chil-*
> *dren according to their several conditions. If he will*
> *make his face to shine upon them, he then makes them*
> *lie down in green pastures and leads them beside the*
> *still waters. If they stick in deep mire and clay, and all*
> *his waves and billows go over their heads, he then leads*
> *them to the rock which is higher than they.*

She had wise words of advice for young mothers:

> *A prudent mother will not clothe her little child with*
> *a long and cumbersome garment; she easily foresees*
> *what events it is likely to produce, at the best but falls*
> *and bruises or perhaps something worse. Much more*
> *will the all-wise God proportion his dispensations ac-*
> *cording to the stature and strength of the person… God*
> *cuts their garments short to keep them in such trim that*
> *they may run the ways of his commandments.*

Left alone to guide her household and discipline her children, Anne learnt many practical lessons from her daily experiences. Sometimes she was at a loss to know what she should do. To whom could she turn for help? In 1639 her parents, Thomas and Dorothy Dudley, had moved from Ipswich to the village of Roxbury, not far from Boston, for Thomas had been chosen as deputy governor once more and needed to be nearer the centre of government.

At such times of solitude Anne discovered in her God her supreme helper and was quick to conclude that his wisdom was infinitely better than even the best earthly advice. God as a heavenly Father knew perfectly how to deal with his children, even if they were wilful and stubborn. So in the discipline of her own family Anne learnt from his chastisements that she too must vary her severity according to the disposition of the individual child.

> *Diverse children have their different natures: some are like flesh [meat] which nothing but salt will keep from putrefaction, some again like tender fruits that are best preserved with sugar. Those parents are wise that can fit their nurture according to their [children's] nature.*

And again, in a similar reflection, she wrote:

> *A wise father will not lay a burden on a child of seven years old which he knows is enough for one of twice his strength; much less will our heavenly Father (who knows our mould) lay such afflictions upon his weak children as would crush them to the dust, but according to the strength he will proportion the load.*

But sometimes there seemed to be no clear solutions to her problems. With Simon far away and no ready means of communication between them, it was easy for her to succumb to anxiety. Often she found herself unable to sleep at night as she wrestled with perplexing situations. But instead of tossing and turning on her bed, she learnt that the best answer was to lie still and turn her heart to God in prayer. In a short poem she describes the result:

> *By night when others soundly slept*
> *and had at once both ease and rest,*
> *my waking eyes were open kept,*
> *and so to lie I found it best.*
>
> *I sought him whom my soul did love,*
> *with tears I sought him earnestly:*

he bowed his ear down from above;
in vain I did not seek or cry.

My hungry soul he filled with good,
he in his bottle put my tears,
my smarting wounds washed in his blood
and banished thence my doubt and fears.

What to my Saviour shall I give,
who freely hath done this for me?
I'll serve him here whilst I shall live
and love him to eternity.

Sometimes Anne's anxieties seemed to persist despite her best efforts to subdue them. Yet it was at such times that her firm confidence in the God on whom she had relied from childhood days proved to be a rock of strength in her need. Was he not the one who had heard her prayer in times of serious illness, who had forgiven her rebellious spirit as she faced dire circumstances, who had granted her a family despite her fears? We may imagine her deep in thought as she walked in the woodland near her home — woods once cleared of tangled undergrowth by Indian fires — with the sunlight slanting between the tall trees; or perhaps she would sit on the shimmering white sands of the beach not far away, watching the distant waves, and so she notes down her meditation in the form of a prayer:

O Lord, let me never forget thy goodness, nor ques-
tion thy faithfulness to me, for thou art my God, thou
hast said, and shall I not believe it? Thou hast given me
a pledge of that inheritance thou hast promised to be-
stow upon me. O never let Satan prevail against me,

but strengthen my faith in thee till I shall attain the end
of my hopes, even the salvation of my soul. Come,
Lord Jesus, come quickly.

Her mind turned to a day when she would praise God without sin and without fear. The thought of the believer as a pilgrim journeying to a better country was always to the fore in Anne's thinking, so now she continues:

But this is my comfort, when I come to heaven, I
shall understand perfectly what he has done for me,
and then I shall praise him as I ought. Lord, having this
hope, let me purify myself as thou art pure, and let me
be no more afraid of death, but even desire to be dis-
solved and be with thee which is best of all.

Yet despite all the spiritual comforts, Anne still missed her husband more than words could express. In a flight of poetic fancy on one occasion, she addresses the sun under the name 'Phoebus' — that same sun that shines on her in Ipswich and also on Simon wherever he might be. She asks the sun to take a message to him from his lonely wife:

Commend me to the man more loved than life,
show him the sorrows of his widowed wife;
my dumpish thoughts, my groans, my brackish tears,
my sobs, my longing hopes, my doubting fears.
And if he love, how can he there abide?
My interest's more than all the world beside…
Tell him I would say more, but cannot well,
oppressed minds abruptest tales do tell.

She urges the sun to hasten with her message and to insist that Simon comes home speedily:

Now post with double speed, mark what I say,
by all our loves, conjure him not to stay.

And it would be good to think of Simon himself surprising his distressed wife as the clatter of hooves is heard on the path, and her long-missed husband dismounts and gives Anne a loving and reassuring kiss.

8.

The two dialogues

He that would keep a pure heart and lead a blameless life must set himself always in the awful presence of God. The consideration of his all-seeing eye will be a bridle to restrain from evil and a spur to quicken on to good duties.

Those words written by Anne Bradstreet sprang directly from her personal experience. Like any Christian, she knew the constant conflict that arises between the sinful desires that still distress a believer and the new life of the Spirit in the soul. And in those days, with her husband Simon so frequently far from home, and with the incessant demands of her young family, Anne often struggled on valiantly and alone against temptations. Self-pity would overwhelm her at times, together with resentment against her circumstances. Sometimes pride and the desire to receive honour for her achievements came over her like a flood.

With her ability to express her inmost thoughts in verse, it was natural that Anne should turn to this medium to convey the struggles she so often faced. Calling her poem

'The Flesh and the Spirit', she imagines a dialogue between twin sisters. Flesh begins by attempting to dash Spirit's hopes of eternal joys, and continues by casting doubt on all those certainties that give a believer courage to tackle each day's problems:

> *Sister, quoth Flesh, what liv'st thou on?*
> *nothing but meditation...*
> *Dost dream of things beyond the moon,*
> *and dost thou hope to dwell there soon?*
> *Art fancy sick, or turned a sot*
> *to catch at shadows which are not?*
> *Come, come, I'll show unto thy sense,*
> *industry hath its recompense...*
> *Dost honour like? Acquire the same*
> *as some to their immortal fame;*
> *and trophies to thy name erect*
> *which wearing time shall ne'er deject.*
> *Earth hath more silver, pearls and gold*
> *than eyes can see or hands can hold.*

These suggestions played on those very temptations with which Anne wrestled, together with the wistful desire to gain recognition for her work, or even renown. But in the words of Flesh's twin sister, Spirit, Anne swiftly counter-attacks these enticing words with a stern rebuke:

> *Be still, thou unregenerate part,*
> *disturb no more my settled heart.*

She sees straight to the root of such pernicious suggestions:

> *For from one father are we not,*
> *thou by old Adam wast begot.*
> *But my arise is from above,*

whence my dear Father I do love…
How oft thy slave, hast thou me made
when I believed what thou hast said…
I'll stop my ears at these thy charms
and count them for my deadly harms.

But Anne's weapons are twofold. Not only can she see the origin of the tempting voice, but she can also see the abundant treasure available in Christ:

How I do live, thou need'st not scoff,
for I have meat thou know'st not of;
the hidden manna I do eat,
the word of life, it is my meat.
My thoughts do yield me more content
than can thy hours in pleasure spent.

More than this, she waits in eager expectation for untold joys to come:

The city where I hope to dwell,
there's none on earth can parallel.
The gates of pearl, both rich and clear,
and angels are for porters there:
the streets thereof transparent gold,
such as no eye did e'er behold.

Anne, who was now about thirty years of age, had already known much sickness and pain in her short life, but the inhabitants of that heavenly city:

From sickness and infirmity
for evermore they shall be free,
nor withering age shall e'er come there,
but beauty shall be bright and clear.

Then, with one last stab at her Flesh's unbelief, Anne ends by declaring roundly:

This city pure is not for thee,
for things unclean there shall not be.

From a small child Anne had experienced much 'sickness and infirmity' and it had left a permanent toll on her health. The smallpox she suffered at the age of fifteen may have caused some disfigurement; the serious bout of illness resembling tuberculosis when she was nineteen had left lifelong debilities, including a degree of lameness which she mentions in her short memoir. As she looked back Anne was able to see God's purposes of correction and mercy behind her trials, but at the time it was far from easy. Tossing and turning on her sickbed in the blistering heat of one New England summer, and without the advantage of modern palliatives, Anne found her afflictions hard to bear. Sometimes even tears could bring no more relief:

In tossing slumbers on my wakeful bed,
bedrenched with tears that flowed from mournful head,
till nature had exhausted all her store,
then eyes lay dry, disabled to weep more.

At such times her only help was in her God, and with an upward look of tearless despair she cried out for help:

And looking up unto his throne on high,
who sendeth help to those in misery,
he chased away those clouds and let me see
my anchor cast i' th' vale with safety.
He eased my soul of woe, my flesh of pain
and brought me to the shore from troubled main.

In addition to her frequent bouts of illness, Anne's regular pregnancies diminished her strength. Much as she loved her ever-increasing family, there was no escaping the demands they placed on her physical reserves. During 1642 Anne's fifth child was born, a daughter whom they named Hannah. Samuel, the eldest, was now aged eight, with Dorothy aged six, Sarah four and Simon just turned two.

In August 1642, soon after Hannah's birth, came news from the home country that left all New England stunned. Civil War had broken out. Their king, Charles I, had raised his standard in Nottingham, declaring hostilities on his own people. The thought of English blood being shed on English ground filled everyone with horror. All knew that this might well lead to fathers being pitted against their sons, and brothers against brothers. Anne's sensitive spirit was dismayed. The Pequot Wars, which had culminated in 1637 when the New England colonists had mercilessly torched a tribal village killing seven to eight hundred defenceless women and children, had been appalling. Here was a further cause of shame and anxiety. Being part of a politically minded family, and having fled their home and country because of the increasing level of unjust taxation and religious persecution, the Bradstreets naturally felt an avid interest in all news that reached their far-flung frontier home in Ipswich.

Reports of a deteriorating situation had been percolating through to the colonies for some time. They had heard of the disdain of the king for parliamentary rights, of the further exorbitant taxes levied from his people. Where would all these things end? With increasing horror New England learnt of Parliament's demand for the execution of the king's right-hand man, Thomas Wentworth, Earl of

King Charles I (1600-1649)

Strafford; then that the House of Lords had passed the Bill of Attainder assigning Strafford to that fatal appointment with the executioner on 22 May 1641. And still the saga continued as even Archbishop Laud himself was impeached by Parliament and imprisoned within the Tower of London. England seemed bent on self-destruction. What would be the implications of these things for the colonies? Would the charter issued by Charles legitimizing their existence be withdrawn by an angry king?

Like most New England colonists, Anne Bradstreet was torn in her loyalties. Although the churches were congregational in their form of government, the leaders of Massachusetts Bay Colony had not severed their links with the Church of England. Nor had they repudiated the authority of Charles as their king appointed by God to rule over them. Yet at the heart of the present conflict were those same issues which had led to their own exile. As a woman Anne had no political influence, nor was she expected to pass any public opinion on the situation, and yet she was burning with unexpressed views. Was there no way in which a woman's voice could be heard?

There was. And as Anne began to put pen to paper, two remarkable things were happening. Without her realizing it, Anne's words would make her the spokesperson for a new nation. New England was coming of age, a separate identity, and these lines were to be a flagship declaration of that fact — the voice of a maturing country which the mother country must recognize. Anne's new work took the form of another dialogue, this time called 'A Dialogue between Old England and New concerning their present troubles, *Anno* 1642'. How little could she have thought that these lines would one day propel her, a little-known colonial woman, to a degree of fame beyond anything she could possibly have imagined! Cast in the imagery of a daughter in conversation with her mother, Anne's stanzas were at once more meaningful, more natural than in any of her earlier work. No longer was she labouring to impress with convoluted sentiments and classical references; here she expressed herself with a degree of abrupt eloquence. The poem opens with New England asking her mother, Old England, in somewhat patronizing tones, what her trouble can be:

Alas, dear Mother, fairest queen and best,
with honour, wealth and peace, happy and blest;
what ails thee...?
What means this wailing tone, this mournful guise?
Ah, tell thy daughter, she may sympathize.

Old England is not impressed by her daughter's ignorance:

Art ignorant indeed of these my woes?
Or must my forcèd tongue these griefs disclose?
And must myself dissect my tattered state?

'You ought to help me,' she insists. 'I need medicines to cure my fearful disease':

If I decease, doth think thou shalt survive?
Or by my wasting state dost think to thrive?

Old England even suggests that her daughter may be secretly rejoicing at her predicament. But New England counters by saying that she cannot suggest a suitable medicine unless her mother tells her what is wrong. Anne's lines then run briefly through English history, naming old enemies, and asking whether they have returned to trouble her mother again. Is it King Canute for a second time? Or perhaps the Norman Conquest threatens once more? Has the Spanish Armada returned? Or is the Dutch nation the problem?

Your humble child entreats you, show your grief
though arms, nor purse she hath for your relief.

But she can at least pray, New England assures her mother. Anne then imagines Old England, encouraged by such kindly words, beginning to acknowledge the way-wardness that had brought about her present distress. These troubles, she confesses, are the punishment for her past sins, which are now being visited on her. At this point in her poem Anne Bradstreet clearly aligns herself with the Puritan cause and allows the mother country to admit the wrongs perpetrated on such loyal citizens as those who had emigrated with her in 1630:

What scorning of the saints of the Most High,
what injuries did daily on them lie?
What false reports, what nicknames did they take
not for their own but for their master's sake?

This was a subtle reference to the nickname 'Puritan' given in mockery to serious-minded Christians. Even the emi-gration of so many to New England for conscience' sake was made the butt of many a joke, as Old England now reveals:

And thou, poor soul, wert jeered among the rest,
thy flying for the truth was made a jest.

Old England had neglected divine warnings:

I mocked the preachers...
that cried destruction to my wicked land;

I then believed not, now I feel and see
the plague of stubborn incredulity.

The mother country's confessions gather pace:

For Sabbath-breaking and for drunkenness
did ever land profaneness more express?

She recalls the fearsome fires of Mary Tudor's reign, consuming some of the finest men and women in her land. As she thinks of such martyrs, she recollects other crimes, especially the grievous death of young Lady Jane Grey, nine-day Queen of England, executed at the age of sixteen:

O Jane, why didst thou die in flow'ring prime?
Because of royal stem, that was thy crime.
For bribery, adultery and lies,
where is the nation I can't paralyse?

Yes, agrees New England, in reply to such confessions, these are certainly heinous offences, but she recognizes that she herself cannot claim to be guiltless:

To all you've said, sad Mother, I assent,
your fearful sins great cause there's to lament,
my guilty hands, in part, hold up with you,
a sharer in your punishment's my due.

But all these things are mere generalities and past misdemeanours. New England now insists that Old England must confess the situation that has led to the present state of affairs and brought about a nation at war with itself:

Pray in plain terms, what is your present grief?
Then let's join heads and hearts for your relief.

Old England immediately dives into the sorry tale:

Well, to the matter then, there's grown of late
'twixt king and peers a question of state,
which is the chief, the law or else the king.
One said, 'It's he,' the other, 'No such thing.'

She continues by describing each step that has led
irrevocably to the calamity of war. Anne is clearly on
Parliament's side as she allows Old England to tell how
'they took high Strafford lower by the head'. Nor is she
impressed to hear how Charles I fled London for York, or
of his constant vacillating with Parliament's many appeals
for some satisfactory resolution. Then Old England confesses the grievous outcome of it all:

But now I come to speak of my disaster,
contention grown 'twixt subjects and their master;
they worded it so long, they fell to blows,
that thousands lay on heaps, here bleeds my woes.

She ends her sad account by begging for New England's
help:

If any pity in thy heart remain,
or any childlike love thou dost retain,
for my relief, do what there lies in thee
and recompense that good I've done to thee.

Now that her mother has made a full confession of all
the steps that have brought about such a fearful state of
affairs, her daughter, New England, steps in with comfort-
ing words, yet words that express clearly Anne's own deep

convictions. 'There is yet hope for you,' she assures Old
England:

> *Your griefs I pity, but soon hope to see*
> *out of your troubles much good fruit to be;*
> *to see those latter days of hoped for good*
> *though now beclouded all with tears and blood.*

In common with much Puritan thought of the time,
Anne held out high expectations of an approaching mil-
lennial bliss soon to dawn in which her benighted homeland would have a share. A day will come, she assures Old
England, when 'dark Popery' will be banished. Then she
will acknowledge those faithful preachers she had previ-
ously despised. The king will reign once more over a
restored and peaceful land; nobles who had sacrificed their
estates, even their lives, will receive the honour due to
them. Then that great day, foretold in Scripture, will be
ushered in when Jew and Gentile will worship side by
side, injustice and error banished for ever:

> *Oh Abraham's seed, lift up your heads on high,*
> *for sure the day of your redemption's nigh;*
> *the scales shall fall from your long blinded eyes,*
> *and him you shall adore who now despise.*
> *Then fulness of the nations in shall flow,*
> *and Jew and Gentile to one worship go.*
> *Then follows days of happiness and rest;*
> *whose lot doth fall to live therein is blest.*

And if such a glorious future awaits Old England, let
her take fresh courage, dry her eyes, and wait on in hope.
With such words of encouragement Anne Bradstreet ends
her dialogue:

Farewell, dear Mother, rightest cause[1] prevail,
And in a while you'll tell another tale.

Anne Bradstreet, unlike that other, less fortunate Anne, Anne Hutchinson, was destined to point the way ahead for both Old England and New in a manner that few other women would have either the opportunity or the ability to achieve.

9.
Into the unknown

News of the unfolding English Civil War, with its sorry tale of disaster and death, was relayed to the colonies through personal correspondence, new arrivals from the troubled homeland and through wild rumours that spread from one settlement to another until it was hard to distinguish truth from error. The stalemate battle at Edgehill in October 1642, the successful manoeuvres of the Royalist troops at Adwalton Moor in June 1643, followed by the Roundaway Down skirmishes the following month when the Parliamentary forces broke rank and fled — such events filled Anne Bradstreet and all her fellow colonists with fear and dismay. What would be the end of these things?

But in December 1643 Anne Bradstreet faced a sorrow in her own family — the sudden death of her mother, Dorothy, at the age of sixty-one. With Anne's sisters, Patience, Sarah and Mercy, all married and absorbed with families of their own, Anne felt the loss acutely. While Patience and Mercy had remained in their frontier settlement of Ipswich,

Sarah had moved to Boston and, to the concern of the whole family, was showing alarming symptoms of instability and erratic behaviour.

As we have seen, Anne's parents had left Ipswich and settled in the village of Roxbury, near Boston, four years earlier. With travel opportunities restricted as a result of her husband's constant absences on colonial business, Anne had seen little of her mother, although Dorothy would have undoubtedly been at hand to help Anne through her numerous confinements. But now to hear of her unexpected heart attack and death on 27 December 1643, and to have had no opportunity to see her once more, was a source of poignant grief.

All Anne could do was to compose a short but sorrowful epitaph in memory of Dorothy. Unassuming, gentle and kind, she had been an ideal of New England womanhood, so Anne could write:

A worthy matron of unspotted life,
a loving mother and obedient wife,
a friendly neighbour, pitiful to poor
whom oft she fed and clothèd with her store...

But, over and above these shining virtues, Dorothy had shown to her family an example of true spiritual life, prayerfulness and consistency. She had 'ordered' her children 'with dexterity', as Anne quaintly expresses it, and even death could not find her totally unready, for she had been 'preparing still for death till end of days'.

Within four months Thomas Dudley, who was now sixty-seven, had remarried. Although this must have eased his sense of loss and reassured his family about his welfare, it can have done little to comfort Anne or her sisters over the death of their mother. Dudley's second wife, Katherine, was a young widow and before long this elderly man found himself the father of another growing family. Meanwhile Anne's life was about to change radically once more. With many of his responsibilities in the colonies now eased, Simon Bradstreet's mind turned towards expanding his own estate, and where better to do so than near the Merrimack River some fifteen miles from Ipswich? John Winthrop's son had bought some land in the area from an Algonquian chief named Cutshamache. He had paid six pounds in the local currency for the land and donated a coat to the Indian chief for good measure. Originally called Chochichawicke, the name of the new plantation was soon changed to Andover, and here Simon proposed to move together with Anne and his five young children.

With Anne pregnant once more, we can well imagine her anxiety as she contemplated a move to an unknown outpost with few of the facilities she had enjoyed in Ipswich. She would have been especially sorry to leave behind her mentor and pastor, Nathaniel Ward. But there was one major consolation. Anne's youngest sister, Mercy, married to a John Woodbridge, had also moved to this lonely outpost. John, a young man with an earnest desire to become a preacher, had undertaken some theological studies at the newly founded Harvard College in order to qualify for such a role. Situated in New Towne (Cambridge), near Anne Bradstreet's home following her move from Charlestown, Harvard was New England's first educational establishment and had been established in 1636 with only nine students. Then known simply as 'the college at New Towne', it was renamed Harvard College in

A view of Harvard in the early days

1639, after a young preacher, John Harvard, who at his death had bequeathed his library of 400 books to the infant institution. Harvard's future eminence would have astonished its founders.

Newly qualified and ordained, John Woodbridge was to become Andover's first preacher, ministering to the settlers in a small meeting house quickly erected for the purpose. So at least Anne would have the comfort in this out-of-the way spot of the presence of her sister and brother-in-law, even though her other sister, Patience, and her family remained in Ipswich. Like Anne, John Woodbridge also had a penchant for writing verse, an interest which naturally forged a closer link between them.

Now in a favoured financial position, Simon Bradstreet was able to contribute generously towards the expenses of establishing the new plantation, a factor which earned him the right to own an extensive area of land in Andover.

Having been granted some twenty acres by the General Court of Massachusetts, his first task was to have it cleared of virgin forest and undergrowth and then to build the spacious home which he planned for Anne and his young family. At last all was ready and in 1646, shortly before the birth of her sixth child, Anne and the family were ready to move.

Meanwhile events in the home country were moving fast. With the creation of the New Model Army, the Parliamentary cause was prevailing and after the Battle of Marston Moor in June 1644 and the Battle of Naseby in June 1645 Royalist resistance had crumbled. Then came the critical moment in the summer of 1646 when Charles himself was captured and imprisoned.

Anne, like many of the colonists with innate loyalty to the Crown, was disturbed by such events, fearing the ultimate outcome. Passages from the book of Ecclesiastes found echoes in her thought: ' "Vanity of vanities, all is vanity," says the preacher.' Nothing seemed certain any more. Turning such reflections into verse, she wrote lines entitled 'The Vanity of all Worldly Things', in which she pondered on the events that had changed not just for her but for her home country, turning her monarch into a mere prisoner of war:

> *Where is the man can say, 'Lo, I have found*
> *on brittle earth a consolation sound'?*
> *What is't in honour to be set on high?*
> *No, they like beasts and sons of men shall die,*
> *and whilst they live, how oft doth turn their fate;*
> *he's now a captive that was king of late.*

But living in such a lonely outpost brought its own concerns to Anne's mind as her confinement approached. The loss of the help of her gentle mother would make her anxieties even more acute. How she missed her, and wished for her presence at this needy moment of her life! All the misgivings and apprehensions to which her sensitive nature was prone rushed through her mind with an added pinch of self-pity. What would Simon do if she died? Would he soon forget her and remarry? Would he keep some memento of his dead wife? If her child survived, who would care for the infant? Would Simon remember only her faults and failings? What would happen to her young family? Would her children be mistreated by a stepmother? All these morbid thoughts found expression in one of her poems:

All things within this fading world hath end,
adversity doth still our joys attend;
no ties so strong, no friends so dear and sweet,
but with death's parting blow is sure to meet...
How soon, my dear, death may my steps attend,
how soon may't be thy lot to lose thy friend? ...
The many faults that well you know I have
let be interred in my oblivious grave.
If any worth or virtue were in me,
let that live freshly in thy memory...
And when thy loss shall be repaid with gains,
look to my little babes, my dear remains.
And if thou love thyself or loved'st me,
these, O protect, from step-dame's injury...
And kiss this paper for thy love's dear sake
who with salt tears this last farewell did take.

Despite her fears, Anne gave birth safely to another daughter, whom they named Mercy, after Anne's sister. Now thirty-four years of age, with six healthy children, a husband she loved dearly and a most attractive home, described in 1650 as 'the showplace of all the countryside', Anne was nevertheless well aware that no amount of earthly good can ultimately satisfy the human spirit — nothing apart from the treasure of spiritual blessedness. And so, concluding her lines on the 'Vanity of all Worldy Things' and thinking of the fugitive king of England, she wrote of a crown that could never be taken away:

> *This pearl of price, this tree of life, this spring,*
> *who is possessed of shall reign a king.*
> *Nor change of state nor cares shall ever see,*
> *but wear his crown unto eternity.*

This same theme, describing the believer as a pilgrim on earth, his earthly life changeful and transient, appears frequently in Anne's writings.

A change of a different sort was shortly to come for Anne Bradstreet, and one she certainly had not expected. With King Charles in captivity, the English Parliament was anxious to find men of moderate opinion, still trusted by the king and yet representing the Puritan position, to negotiate with him, aiming to persuade him to accept a reasonable compromise with his victorious subjects. One man, known and loved by Anne, was summoned to London to take part in these delicate negotiations — her own brother-in-law John Woodbridge. Also her close adviser and former pastor Nathaniel Ward decided to return to England at the same time to help in the present crisis in any way he could. At seventy years of age, he felt his usefulness in New England drawing to a close. Anne realized that he would never return and must have grieved at the loss of his friendship and advice.

How John Woodbridge managed to persuade his sister-in-law Anne to lend him copies of all her manuscript poems before he left we do not know. Perhaps he asked if he could read her work at leisure during the long weeks at sea during the voyage to England. Among the manuscripts she lent him she had included the four long quaternions, on the Elements, the Temperaments (or Constitutions), the Seasons and the Ages of Man. Most importantly, however, 'A Dialogue between Old England and New' was there and also various elegies and shorter pieces.

Another manuscript she included was entitled 'The Four Monarchies' — a new and lengthy poem not quite finished. This was a brave attempt to chronicle the history of the ancient world. Written in rhyming couplets, and running to approximately 3,500 lines, Anne's epic began, 'When time was young and world in infancy...' With Babel and Nineveh as a starting point, she attempted an account of the first significant world dynasty, the Assyrian. Next came the history of the Persian Empire, then the Grecian and lastly the Roman. Drawing on the extensive classical education she had received during her childhood in Lincolnshire, Anne displayed a prodigious knowledge of her subject. She had set out on this impressive work before the family left Ipswich and while she still had access to Nathaniel Ward's books, in addition to the growing reference library owned by her husband, Simon. But with the upheaval of the move to Andover, followed by the birth of her baby, she had laid the work aside. In her final section dealing with Roman history, Anne had reached no further than the reign of the last Roman king, Tarquinius Superbus, more commonly known as Tarquin, whose violence-filled time in power had ended with his exile in 509 BC. This would be followed by the establishment of the republic, but Anne had not yet arrived at that point. Her mammoth *tour de force* still lay unfinished on her desk when her brother-in-law John Woodbridge asked to 'borrow' her manuscripts. These he carefully packed away among his belongings and stepped aboard a vessel bound for England.

10.

'My rambling brat'

John Woodbridge and those assigned to negotiate with
Charles I found it a frustrating and ultimately a useless
task. With a streak of obstinacy in his character, the king
prevaricated endlessly and seemed totally unwilling to
consider any compromise settlement with his subjects.
Described as the 'Grand Delinquent', Charles managed
repeatedly to evade the burning issues of the day, and at
last gave his captors the slip by escaping from Hampton
Court Palace, where he was being held in custody. Re-
arrested on the Isle of Wight, Charles still resisted all
further attempts at negotiation.

Dismayed, but remaining hopeful, John Woodbridge,
Nathaniel Ward and others continued their efforts to
reason with the king during his imprisonment in Caris-
brooke Castle. But, without their knowledge, Charles was
engaging in secret negotiations of his own, not with Parliament and the victorious army, but with his Scottish
subjects. He agreed to their demands that a Presbyterian
church system should be established in Scotland, at least

temporarily. In return they would raise arms on his behalf in an attempt to restore him to his throne. Because of this underhand deal Charles was responsible for a renewed outbreak of war in the country. In April 1648 the Scots invaded northern England and Royalist supporters in Wales and elsewhere, already on the brink of revolt and heartened by this success, joined in the armed combat.

John Woodbridge could see that his role as an intermediary was over, at least for the time being, but did not feel it right to return to Massachusetts as yet. In view of the current uncertainty he decided to send for his wife Mercy and the children to join him in England until he was convinced that he could play no further part in the sorry saga that was enveloping his home country.

Meanwhile back in Massachusetts Anne Bradstreet faced a period of considerable loneliness. Her husband Simon was still often away on business, some of it connected with the sawmill — which was of vital importance at a time when many homes were made all of wood — and the farm which he was then developing in Andover. With Mercy and John now far off in England, her mother dead and her father wrapped up in the affairs of the colony and of his new family, Anne sometimes felt acutely isolated. Her growing family and the bustling household clearly engrossed much of her attention, but she had few with whom she felt able to share her inmost thoughts. Her son Samuel, the eldest in the family, was now fourteen and away at school, and just one year after the birth of her own little Mercy, Anne found herself pregnant yet again. Physically she was already exhausted after frequent illness and six earlier pregnancies. Some of the poems written not long after the birth of her seventh child, named Dudley

after her father, reflect her cry to God for his help in her
need:

> Worthy art thou, O Lord, of praise,
> but ah! it's not in me!
> My sinking heart I pray thee raise,
> so shall I give it thee.

And it was a prayer God heard, for she continues:

> My feeble spirit thou didst revive,
> my doubting thou didst chide.
> And though as dead mad'st me alive.
> I here a while might 'bide.

However low she felt, Anne knew that the only real
satisfaction must come from any service she could offer to
her God:

> Why should I live but to thy praise?
> My life is hid with thee.
> O Lord, no longer be my days
> than I may fruitful be.

Yet far off in England a situation was developing with
regard to Anne's poems in John Woodbridge's possession
that would show her that God still had purposes for her
life. As negotiations with the king were at a standstill, John
had decided that the time was right for him to devote his
attention to finding a publisher for his sister-in-law's verse.
In keeping with the protocol of the day, the first step was
to obtain sponsors who would be happy to recommend the
work.

This could be a long and laborious task. The first problem was to make sure that no reader kept the manuscripts for an inordinate length of time, but was able to write a commendation without too much delay. However, a far greater problem was the fact that this was the work of a woman. Some readers would not believe it possible that any woman could compose such striking, vibrant and rounded lines of historical and classical content and therefore would discount it for that reason. In his 'Epistle to the Reader', John's eulogy on Anne's virtues was liberal, if a little extreme:

> *I doubt not but the reader will quickly find more than I can say [in these verses], and the worst effect of his reading will be unbelief, which will make him question whether it be a woman's work, and ask, is it possible? If any do, take this answer from him that dares avow it: it is the work of a woman, honoured and esteemed where she lives, for her gracious demeanour ... her pious conversation, her courteous disposition, her exact diligence in her place, and discreet management of her family.*

Nathaniel Ward quickly joined Woodbridge in his attempt to publish Anne's work. Although known for his low estimate of women in general, he was even stauncher than Woodbridge in his support for Anne's poetry. In a convoluted compliment he suggested that if the Greek god Apollo himself were to be shown Anne's poetry and at the same time that of Guillaume du Bartas, whom Anne had taken as her poetic model, he would not be able to decide which was the better of the two.

And then Ward commented drolly:

I muse whither at length these girls will go;
it half revives my chill frost-bitten blood
to see a woman once do aught that's good;
and shod by Chaucer's boots, and Homer's furs,
let men look to't, lest women wear the spurs.

Eleven sponsors were found willing to add their commendations to the volume, most prepared to be identified only by their initials. A certain 'H. S.' wrote:

I've read your poem, Lady, and admire
your sex to such a pitch should e'er aspire;
go on to write, continue to relate
new histories, of monarchy and state:
and what the Romans to their poets gave,
be sure such honour and esteem you'll have.

All that remained was to find a publisher willing to take the risk of accepting such a work. And here again Anne's friend and former pastor Nathaniel Ward had the answer. His own book, *The Simple Cobbler of Aggawam*, which had been published in 1647, under the pseudonym Theodore de la Guard, had proved highly popular reading and had gone swiftly through four printings.

In a pithy satire, Ward portrays his convictions under the imagery of a cobbler seeking to repair old England's woes as a cobbler would a worn pair of shoes. One of the main thrusts of his jocular narrative was a diatribe against any toleration for those of differing religious persuasions. Perhaps he had forgotten that his fellow colonists had fled to New England in search of just such toleration for their convictions. He also insisted that the king must be restored to his throne. Still in print today, Ward's *Simple Cobbler* also

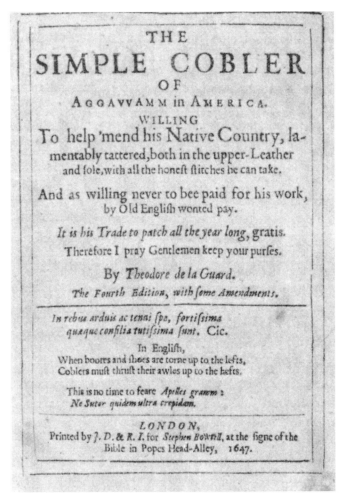

Title page of 'The Simple Cobbler of Aggawam'

reveals his deeply compassionate nature and spiritual
strengths.

With his own work so popular, Ward suggested that his
publisher, Stephen Bowtell, might be well disposed towards any title that he recommended. And so the manuscript of Anne Bradstreet's work passed from Woodbridge

to Bowtell — but not before an event of cataclysmic proportions, a national watershed, occurred on 30 January 1649. The King of England was executed.

All negotiations had failed, and Charles had not been willing to consider any compromise which would limit his powers under a new constitutional settlement. But his final offence had been the act of inciting the Scots to raise an army in his defence in 1648, thus provoking a second civil war and causing further fearful bloodshed and divisions in the land. Accused of high treason, the king had been brought to trial in St James Palace, London, but refused to enter a defence, regarding any court attempting to put their monarch on trial as illegitimate. His death stunned the nation.

When news of the execution reached that far-away outpost in Andover, Massachusetts, Anne was saddened and horrified. Although no friend of the king's policies towards those of her persuasion, at heart she supported the monarchy. She also realized how her friends Nathaniel Ward and John Woodbridge must be feeling. Most Puritans were of the view that rebellion against 'the powers that be', however great the provocation, was contrary to the Scriptures.[1] One aim of Ward's book had been to avert any dire outcome to the maelstrom of the Civil War into which England had been plunged. With verse as her natural medium of expression, Anne decided to write a barely concealed memorial to Charles which she hastily sent to her friends, probably by way of consolation. Choosing as her theme the death of Saul and Jonathan on Mount Gilboa and David's mournful dirge when he received the news, she wrote memorable lines:

Alas, slain is the head of Israel,
illustrious Saul, whose beauty did excel;
upon thy places mountainous and high,
how did the mighty fall, and falling die? ...
For there the mighty ones did soon decay,
the shield of Saul was vilely cast away,
there had his dignity so sore a foil,
as if his head ne'er felt the sacred oil.

Quickly including this poem in the collection now in the hands of Stephen Bowtell, John Woodbridge had little else to do other than decide upon a suitable title for Anne's work. Then an idea struck him. Anne had referred to the nine Muses in the prologue to her poems. Greek mythology claimed that Zeus, father of the gods, had nine daughters who were said to be the inspiration behind all the arts and sciences, with one, Calliope, in particular, as the goddess of poetry. If the Greeks had not despised the gifts of women, Anne had reasoned, why should we?

But sure the antique Greeks were far more mild,
else of our sex, why feigned they those nine
and poesy made Calliope's own child;
so 'mongst the rest they placed the arts divine?

Then, thought John Woodbridge, why not call Anne Bradstreet herself 'The Tenth Muse'? And so it was decided, and all without Anne's own knowledge.

In July 1650 *The Tenth Muse — lately sprung up in America* took the English reading public by surprise. Measuring less than six inches in height and with diminutive print, this first volume to be given over entirely to a woman's poetry began to circulate. But John Woodbridge had a problem. He had acted without Anne's permission,

THE
TENTH MUSE

Lately fprung up in AMERICA.

OR

Severall Poems, compiled
with great variety of VVit
and Learning, full of delight.
Wherein efpecially is contained a compleat difcourfe and defcription of

The Four
- *Elements,*
- *Conftitutions,*
- *Ages of Man,*
- *Seafons of the Year.*

Together with an Exact Epitomie of
the Four Monaichies, *viz.*

The
- *Affyrian,*
- *Perfian,*
- *Grecian,*
- *Roman.*

Alfo a Dialogue between Old *England* and
New, concerning the late troubles.
With divers other pleafant and ferious Poems.

By a Gentlewoman in thofe parts.

Printed at London for *Stephen Bowtell* at the figne of the
Bible in Popes Head-Alley. 1650.

Title page of 'The Tenth Muse'

and might well face his sister-in-law's indignation. In his preface he admits:

> I fear the displeasure of no person in the publishing of these poems but the author, without whose knowledge and contrary to her expectation, I have presumed to bring to public view what she resolved should (in such a manner) never see the sun.

The reception of *The Tenth Muse* was euphoric. War-weary, uncertain of the future and troubled, the English people were both diverted and encouraged by the novelty of a woman who could write excellent poetry. Better still, Anne's strong Christian faith shone through her lines, even though she had not set out to write religious verse. Her message of hope in the closing lines of 'A Dialogue between Old England and New' gave her readers fresh confidence that God would order the chaotic events engulfing the land so that right should at last prevail. A day would come, so Anne predicted, when:

> ... justice shall in all thy courts take place,
> without respect of persons or of case,
> then bribes shall cease, and suits shall not stick long,
> patience and purse of clients oft to wrong...
> So shall thy happy nation ever flourish
> when truth and righteousness they thus shall nourish.

Public demand soon resulted in multiple printings as *The Tenth Muse* was passed from hand to hand. Gradually letters began to arrive in New England congratulating Anne on her achievement — the first she had heard of it. Then came a small parcel bringing Anne her very own first copy. We can imagine the trepidation with which she tore off the wrappings and turned over the small leather-bound volume in her hand. Undoubtedly she experienced a fleeting sense of pleasure at the sight, but this was quickly followed by acute dismay when she realized that here, beyond her powers of recall, lay her *unedited* work, littered with mistakes, both her own and those of the printer, marring any sense of satisfaction.

Rarely can a poet have felt more embarrassed and distressed as she turned the pages, not because her work had been published, but because of its glaring short-comings, which to the eye of the writer seemed to loom larger than those astonishing qualities which had taken English readers by storm. All Anne could do now was to set about working on a corrected version which she hoped might appear in any second edition if one should ever be printed. Referring to *The Tenth Muse* under the imagery of an 'ill-formed offspring' who had been grabbed away from his mother's side, she describes her feelings:

Thou ill-formed offspring of my feeble brain,
who after birth didst by my side remain,
till snatched from thence by friends, less wise than true,
who thee abroad, exposed to public view.

Her mortification as she looked through the book is vividly described:

At thy return my blushing was not small,
my rambling brat (in print) should mother call.

She could scarcely bear to recognize such a 'brat' as her own:

I cast thee by as one unfit for light,
thy visage was so irksome in my sight.

But, despite her dismay, *The Tenth Muse* was indeed her
own work, and once Anne had recovered from the shock
she describes her efforts at improvement:

I washed thy face, but more defects I saw,
and rubbing off a spot still made a flaw.

It was hard work and even after her best efforts she was
far from satisfied:

In better dress to trim thee was my mind,
but nought but homespun cloth i' th' house I find.

At length, with a measure of despair, she tells her
'offspring' that she can do no more and must send him off
again, but warns him to beware of allowing himself to
come under any critic's stern gaze, concluding with one
further warning for her 'brat':

If for thy father asked, say thou hadst none,
and for thy mother, she alas is poor,
which caused her thus to send thee out of door.

Many years would pass before John and Mercy Woodbridge returned to New England, so he escaped his sister-
in-law's immediate indignation, and an evidence of the
affection remaining between them is suggested by the
choice of the name 'John' for her eighth and last child, born
in 1652.

11.
Strength in weakness

If Anne Bradstreet was ever tempted to a degree of pride in her achievements, this was counterbalanced in two ways. First, she had a strong sense of her indebtedness to God for any gift she possessed and the realization that a day was coming when she must give an account of all that she had done with that gift. But added to this, during the five years following the publication of *The Tenth Muse* Anne experienced a period of almost unremitting illness, sapping her strength and causing her to turn to God continually for his help and healing.

Many Christians can testify that before a period of unusual trial they had a special awareness of God's love and grace which has strengthened and sustained them in their need. And this was Anne's experience. Often lonely and struggling to cope with all the demands of her large family, she describes a time 'when my soul has been refreshed with consolations which the world knows not'. Perhaps she had been walking alone by the river or through the woods, or more realistically was at home surrounded by her noisy, clamouring family. Whether alone or not, she was privileged with a unique and memorable disclosure of God's character and presence. She may well have been wrestling against a recurrence of those doubts and anxieties which had troubled her in earlier years, but this fresh encounter with the one whom she had trusted from childhood days dispelled her doubts and supported her with assurances of his love and faithfulness. Expressing her thoughts in the form of a prayer, she writes:

> *Lord, why should I doubt any more when thou hast given me such assured pledges of thy love? First, thou art my Creator, I thy creature. Thou art my Father, I thy child ... but lest this should not be enough, 'Thy Maker is thy husband' [Isaiah 54:5]. Nay more, I am a member of his body, he is my head... So wonderful are these thoughts that my spirit fails in me at the consideration thereof, and I am confounded to think that God, who has done so much for me, should have so little from me. But this is my comfort, when I come to heaven I shall understand perfectly what he has done for me.*

In previous times of illness the fear of death had often haunted her. What would her young family do without her? But now, even though her youngest, John, was little more than a year old and Dudley not yet five, this confirmation of the intimate relationship between God and his people drove out such terrors until she could write, 'Let me be no more afraid of death, but even desire to be dissolved and be with thee, which is best of all.'

Shortly after this the family had a further taste of bereavement when Anne's father, Thomas Dudley, died on 31 July 1653 at the age of seventy-seven. Exactly ten years had elapsed since her mother, Dorothy, had died, and although Anne had probably not been as close to her father since his re-

Thomas Dudley (1576–1653)

marriage, she felt his loss deeply. From her early days he had given her the best educational advantages possible and encouraged her talent. He had been 'my father, guide, instructor too', Anne wrote in an elegy to his memory. She had sincerely respected him, but perhaps feared him as well. With a hard streak in his nature, he had alienated many, particularly those who were less rigid than himself, men like John Winthrop. But his faithfulness to the truth as he perceived it was unwavering:

> *Truth's friend thou wert, to errors still a foe,*
> *which caused apostates to malign so.*
> *Thy love to true religion e'er shall shine,*
> *my father's God be God to me and mine.*

Although he had been 'to sectaries a whip' (men like Roger Williams had felt the lash), as a public servant her father was second to none, in Anne's opinion. Certainly he had served as governor of Massachusetts Bay Colony on four separate occasions and had signed the founding

Charter for the founding of Harvard College signed by Thomas Dudley

charter for Harvard College. Even today a gate at Harvard bears his name. However, one virtue above others shone out in Anne's eyes: he had not attempted to build up a fine estate for himself in the New World, but was always a pilgrim at heart — a characteristic less true of Anne's own husband Simon, who was a born businessman.

> *Upon the earth he did not build his nest,*
> *but as a pilgrim what he had, possessed.*
> *High thoughts he gave no harbour in his heart,*
> *nor honours puffed him up when he had part;*
> *those titles loathed which some too much do love,*
> *for truly his ambition lay above.*

With such a pilgrim spirit Dudley too had lost the fear of death and even spoke of his approaching end without a tremor. Like wheat gathered into the barn, Anne assures her readers, he had no dread of winter storms. With overstatement typical of the times, Anne eulogized her father:

Ah happy soul, 'mongst saints and angels blest,
who after all his toil is now at rest:
his hoary head in righteousness is found,
as joy in heaven, on earth let praise resound.
Forgotten never be his memory,
his blessing rest on his posterity:
his pious footsteps followed by his race,
at last will bring us to that happy place
where we with joy each other's face shall see,
and parted more by death shall never be.

As we have seen, Anne's own health was precarious at this time. The birth of eight children had left her strength at a low ebb. With a small physical frame and a catalogue of previous health problems, she entered her forties at a disadvantage in terms of fitness. In her poems at this time she describes the symptoms of her recurring condition, characteristic of a severe attack of influenza:

My burning flesh in sweat did boil,
my aching head did break,
from side to side for ease I toil,
so faint I could not speak.

As so often happens in any prolonged period of illness, Anne's spirits became depressed and low. She imagined that in some way she must have incurred God's displeasure and consequently began to lose the assurance of her salvation:

Beclouded was my soul with fear
of thy displeasure sore,
nor could I read my evidence
which oft I read before.

But in her need she cried out to God for help and mercy:

Hide not thy face from me, I cried,
from burnings keep my soul.
Thou know'st my heart, and hast me tried;
I on thy mercies roll.

And it was a cry that God heard, first by giving her a
new assurance that all was well with her soul, and then by
granting her a further measure of physical healing:

Thou heard'st, thy rod thou didst remove
and spared my body frail,
thou show'st to me thy tender love,
my heart no more might quail.
O praises to my mighty God!
Praise to my Lord, I say,
who has redeemed my soul from pit,
praises to him for aye.

Almost all of Anne Bradstreet's poems that have survived from these years deal with this single theme of
illness, leading to despair, followed by earnest prayer and
recovery and thanksgiving. Not once but many times over,
this mother of eight succumbed to serious infections and in
her weakness and suffering begged God for his healing
and mercy. On 8 July 1656 her illness was compounded by
the fact that once again Simon was away from home.
Feeling bereft and with a degree of self-pity and chagrin,

she decided that her condition had been 'so much the sorer … because my dear husband was from home (who is my chiefest comforter on earth)'. But, she adds hastily, 'My God who never failed me was not absent but helped me and graciously manifested his love to me.'

Yet, in case her words appeared to be a criticism of Simon, she insists that she was writing this to fortify herself and others in any future time of illness and similar need. Even so, Satan had tried to take advantage of the situation to such an extent that she expressed a wish to die that she might escape from these trials. But, however buffeted, the foundation of Anne's faith remained sure, and she became content to await God's purposes for her life, looking forward in hope for that time when Christ should either return again or else take her to himself.

With renewed confidence in Christ, she now laid down a challenge to those who dared to belittle the God who comes to the aid of his people:

> *Go, worldings to your vanities,*
> *and heathen to your gods;*
> *let them help in adversities,*
> *and sanctify their rods.*

Her God, she insisted, would never abandon his children in their need. He had pledged to give them eternal life and was true to his word:

> *He is not man that he should lie,*
> *nor son of man to unsay;*
> *his word he plighted hath on high,*
> *and I shall live for aye.*

Even though Anne had been faithfully taught from childhood that her afflictions and sorrows were allowed by God in order to discipline, train and bring her into a closer relationship with himself, it was a lesson that she found she must learn many times over, and never more so than in this prolonged period of sickness. As she would write in August 1656, when her youngest child John was now four years of age, and she herself forty-four:

> *After much weakness and sickness when my spirits were worn out, and many times my faith weak likewise, the Lord was pleased to uphold my drooping heart, and to manifest his love to me, and this is that which stays my soul: that this condition that I am in is the best for me, for God does not afflict willingly, nor take delight in grieving the children of men: he has no benefit in my adversity nor is he the better for my prosperity, but he does it for my advantage, and that I may be the gainer by it. And if he knows that weakness and a frail body is the best to make me a vessel fit for his use, why should I not bear it not only willingly but joyfully?*

At this very time Anne was receiving adulation on every side for her poetry published in *The Tenth Muse*. Demand in England ran high, with her work, described as one of the most saleable books on the market, being purchased alongside such classics as John Milton's works, poems by George Herbert and even Shakespeare's sonnets. Eulogies from admirers and letters from fans poured into Andover, possibly lying unopened while Anne herself tossed to and fro on her bed with a high fever. Struggling with depression and weakness, she could still cry out humbly to God:

Lord, grant that while I live I may do that service I am able in this frail body, and be in continual expect-ation of my change, and let me never forget thy great love to my soul so lately expressed, when I could lie down and bequeath my soul to thee and death seemed no terrible thing.

Recovering once again, she wrote in moving lines:

My winter's past, my storms are gone,
and former clouds seem now all fled,
but if they must eclipse again,
I'll run where I was succourèd.

I have a shelter from the storm,
a shadow from the fainting heat,
I have access unto his throne,
who is a God so wondrous great.

12.

Eight chicks in a nest

After five years of intermittent fevers between 1652 and 1657, Anne Bradstreet unexpectedly found her health much improved. The burden of her young family had been sapping her energy, but now the situation was easing. As thankfulness to God welled up within her for renewing her strength, Anne turned as usual to the medium of verse to express her praise:

> *What shall I render to my God*
> *for all his bounty showed to me?*
> *Even for his mercies in his rod,*
> *where pity most of all I see...*
> *Thy name and praise to celebrate,*
> *O Lord, for aye is my request.*
> *O grant I do it in this state,*
> *and then with thee, which is the best.*

Anne would soon experience a trial of a different sort, however — a long separation from her eldest son, Samuel. When the young man decided that he must travel to England to complete his medical studies, his mother was perturbed. When would she see him again? What dangers might he meet on the Atlantic crossing? Who would care for him in a land where he was a stranger? Such anxieties went round and round in her mind. In point of fact few vessels actually came to any disaster on such a voyage, but Anne's imagination tormented her with fear of other dangers, such as food shortages and pirates, ever-present on the high seas. When Samuel embarked on his long journey on 6 November 1657, only one course remained for this troubled mother, and Anne was quick to avail herself of it: she turned her anxieties into prayer. She reminded God of her earnest requests before the birth of this son, of his gift of the child. She now resigned him to God's care:

Thou mighty God of sea and land,
I here resign into thy hand
the son of prayers, of vows, of tears,
the child I stayed for many years.
Thou heard'st me then and gav'st him me;
hear me again, I give him thee.
He's mine, but more, O Lord, thine own,
for sure thy grace on him is shown.

She continues by seeking God's preserving care over Samuel in whatever dangers or need he might find himself and asking that he might be brought back to her in safety. But she also accepts God's purposes even if they should prove adverse to her wishes.

Writing two years later, in June 1659, Anne gives a memorable and quaint description of her family life. Under the sustained imagery of a mother bird with her brood of nestlings, she describes the present position and the prospects of her eight children:

Anne Bradstreet with her brood of 'nestlings', as depicted in a stained-glass window in St Botolph's Church, Boston, Lincolnshire.

I had eight birds hatched in one nest,
four cocks there were, and hens the rest.
I nursed them up with pain and care,
nor cost, nor labour did I spare,
till at the last they felt their wing,
mounted the trees and learnt to sing.

Almost two years had passed since Samuel had 'felt his wings' and set sail for England. Anne had constantly missed him:

Chief of the brood then took his flight
to regions far and left me quite.
My mournful chirps I after send,
till he return or I do end.

Of her two older girls, Dorothy, now aged twenty-three, had married John Cotton's son, named Seaborn because of his birth at sea during the voyage from Boston in England to Boston, Massachusetts. She and Seaborn had first settled in Wethersfield, Connecticut, and then moved to New Hampshire. Dorothy, an exceptionally attractive-looking young woman, was now also far away and Anne felt the absence of this second 'nestling' acutely:

My second bird did take her flight
and with her mate flew out of sight.
Southward they both their course did bend,
and seasons twain they there did spend,
till after blown by southern gales
they nor'ward steered with fillèd sails.

Sarah, aged twenty-one, had just married Richard Hubbard, a well-to-do businessman, who was well able to provide handsomely for her. Anne was glad that the couple had settled in nearby Ipswich, only fifteen miles distant from Andover:

> *I have a third of colour white*
> *on whom I placed no small delight,*
> *coupled with mate loving and true*
> *hath also bid her dam adieu;*
> *and where Aurora first appears [i.e. the east coast],*
> *she now hath perched to spend her years.*

Anne and Simon Bradstreet's second son, their fourth child, also called Simon, was one to whom his mother would remain close for the rest of her life. Perhaps the nineteen-year-old fulfilled her heart's desire more than her other sons for, after studying at Harvard, he was now preparing to enter the Christian ministry. This was the foremost desire of a New England Puritan woman for her son, although there is no evidence that either Anne or Simon had put any pressure on their boys to follow such a course. Her next lines refer to the progress of her fourth 'chick':

> *One to the Academy flew*
> *to chant among that learned crew:*
> *ambition moves still in his breast*
> *that he might chant above the rest,*
> *striving for more than to do well,*
> *that nightingales he might excel.*

With eleven-year-old Dudley away at school in Ipswich, Anne writes of 'my other three' who were still at home. These included her daughter Hannah, now seventeen, who was doubtless looking out for some marriageable young man, or perhaps already eyeing Andrew Wiggin hopefully. Mercy was thirteen, and John not yet seven.

Like Christian mothers in every generation Anne Bradstreet followed each of her children with her prayers and even tears:

> *If birds could weep then would my tears*
> *let others know what are my fears*
> *lest this my brood some harm should catch*
> *and be surprised for want of watch.*

As in our own day, snares for the young were all around, and Anne feared for her family. Maintaining the imagery of the perils awaiting unwary baby birds as soon as they leave the nest, Anne trembles lest:

> *Whilst pecking corn and void of care*
> *they fall un'wares in fowler's snare,*
> *or whilst on trees they sit and sing,*
> *some untoward boy at them do fling.*

She enumerates various other hazards that might befall her young and then, taking her imagery to an almost comical level, she recalls her care whilst they were in the 'nest':

> *Great was my pain when I you bred,*
> *great was my care when I you fed,*
> *long did I keep you soft and warm*
> *and with my wings kept off all harm.*

Now that some of her brood were beyond her immediate care her anxieties were not lessened; rather they had become more intense:

My cares are more and fears than ever,
my throbs such now as 'fore were never.
Alas! my birds, you wisdom want,
of perils you are ignorant...
O to your safety have an eye
so happy you may live and die.

Mindful of all her recent severe illnesses, Anne was well aware that she might not have many years left to live. But while she was still with them she would give her family as much care and advice as she was able. Nor would she mourn the passing years:

My age I will not once lament,
but sing, my time so near is spent...

Soon that day would come when she would leave them for ever and, like a migrating bird:

... take my flight
into a country beyond sight,
and there with seraphim set song.

But meanwhile her 'birds' would be busy building nests of their own and raising their own broods of chicks. With a degree of pathos Anne asks her young to remember her when she has gone and to tell their offspring 'in chirping language' that she:

... did what could be done for young
and nursed you up till you were strong,
and 'fore she once would let you fly
she showed you joy and misery...

This poem was designed to remind her family of the mother they had lost:

Thus gone, amongst you I may live,
and dead yet speak, and counsel give:
Farewell, my birds, farewell, adieu,
I happy am if well with you.

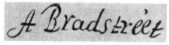

Anne Bradstreet's signature

Unlike most of her poems, Anne signed these charming and personal lines with her initials. They were to be her legacy, a memorial, in the event of her death and were to bring to her children's minds those principles of life and faith which she had attempted to inculcate into their hearts and those warnings she had constantly given.

Meanwhile a situation of critical proportions was developing in England. The Lord Protector, Oliver Cromwell, had died on 3 September 1658. Once more the country was plunged into turmoil as Richard Cromwell, Oliver's kindly, though inadequate gentleman son, struggled to keep the warring factions of the army and the Rump Parliament from active conflict with one another. The country might well be heading for a fresh civil war. Then in 1660 news reached Massachusetts that the executed king's son, also named Charles, was being recalled from exile and offered his father's throne.

These things might well affect the status of the entire Massachusetts Bay Colony. It was vital that some of their ablest men should travel at once to England to make representations on behalf of the colony in the court of the new king, persuading him that the colony was in no way a threat to his crown. Anne had few illusions as to who might be chosen to undertake these delicate negotiations. Her father, Thomas Dudley, was dead, so too were John Winthrop and John Cotton, and Nathaniel Ward had returned to England some years earlier. Simon Bradstreet was an obvious choice to head up the delegation.

Even though it was midwinter, with relentless storms and icy seas, Simon must go and on 16 January 1661 he set sail. All Anne could now do was to commit the situation to God in prayer:

Into thy everlasting arms
of mercy I commend
thy servant, Lord, keep and preserve
my husband, my dear friend.

She prayed for support for herself:

Uphold my heart in thee, O God,
thou art my strength and stay,
thou see'st how weak and frail I am,
hide not thy face away.

She prayed for God's protecting hand over Simon as he travelled:

Lord, be thou pilot to the ship,
and send them prosperous gales,
in storms and sickness, Lord, preserve,
thy goodness never fails.

And that Simon might be prospered in his endeavour and come back to her safely, she prayed:

Lord, let my eyes see once again
him whom thou gavest me

that we together may sing praise
for ever unto thee.

No sooner had Simon's ship disappeared from view
than Anne was taken ill once more with that same condition that had brought her low four years earlier. Perhaps
her anxiety over Simon's difficult mission, with no certain
hope of his early return, made her more vulnerable to in-
fection. Once again her weakness cast her on her God. Four
long months would pass before she recovered strength,
months in which she cried ceaselessly for healing and
renewed vigour. And with the return of health in May 1661
she reached swiftly for her pen to record her thankfulness:

Lord, whilst my fleeting time shall last,
thy goodness let me tell,
and new experience I have gained
my future doubts repel.

And now her prayer was that her gratitude should be
demonstrated not by words alone, but by a closer walk
with God:

A humble, faithful life, O Lord,
for ever let me walk;
let my obedience testify
my praise lies not in talk.

But Anne's trials were also mitigated by great joy. In
that same month, May 1661, she received news that her son
Samuel was coming home, possibly at the express instruc-
tion of his father, who had arrived in England by this time.
When the ship drew in to Boston Harbour on 17 July 1661,
Anne raised a paean of praise to her God for his mercies:

All praise to him who hath now turned
fears to joys, my sighs to song,
my tears to smiles, my sad to glad:
he's come, for whom I waited long.

Nor had the journey been uneventful, for a storm of
fearsome proportions had hit the small vessel, tossing it
about like flotsam on the waves. A nearby ship had foun-
dered and sunk without trace. Then a narrow escape from
pirates ensued, adding to the catalogue of near disasters:

From dangers great thou didst him free
of pirates who were near at hand,
and order'st so the adverse wind
that he before them got to land.

When Samuel reached Andover he had much to tell his
mother. Anne could always see the hand of her God as the
first cause for every event. So now she praised him for his
many mercies to Samuel. He had raised up unexpected
help for her son when he was in need and a stranger. He
had healed him when an epidemic of some deadly illness
had swept through the area where he was living. While
others all around were dying, including members of the
royal family, Samuel had recovered and Anne could
celebrate God's own interventions and mercy:

In sickness when he lay full sore,
his help and his physician wert,
when royal ones that time did die,
thou healed'st his flesh and cheered his heart.

Yes, God had heard and abundantly answered all the prayers she had offered for her absent son. With full heart she could exclaim:

On eagles' wings him hither brought
through want and dangers manifold,
and thus hath granted my request
that I thy mercies might behold.

So now she prayed that she might fulfil those vows made to God in her time of need:

O help me pay my vows, O Lord,
that ever I may thankful be.

And her prayer for Samuel was that he too might realize how God had intervened on his behalf, and that God might:

… in both our hearts erect a frame
of duty and of thankfulness,
that all thy favours great received
our upright walking may express.

To this poem of gratitude Anne added an unusual footnote: 'O Lord, grant that I may never forget thy loving kindness in this particular, and how graciously thou hast answered my desires.'

13.
Gathering clouds

All London had gone mad — or so it must have seemed to Simon Bradstreet, recently arrived in England, as he stood watching the expressions of ecstasy on the faces of the people celebrating the coronation of their new king, Charles II. Simon's visit had coincided with that day in April 1661 when, with splendid pomp and magnificent ceremony, England crowned its king. Fountains played; cannons roared their greeting; bands of music set at intervals along the royal route rang out in jubilation; jewels of inestimable value sparkled on the garments of all the stately attendants. And as for the cheering masses, to them it seemed that the long years of despair, strife and slaughter were gone for ever. But for Simon himself, squeezed in among the crowds, the situation appeared far less sanguine. True, he had been glad to see the monarchy restored, but the success of his mission to persuade the new king to ratify the charter granted to the colony by his father Charles I was far from certain.

Charles II (1630–1685)

Meanwhile his wife Anne, back in Andover, Massachusetts, was finding the days long and lonely. She missed Simon badly, and many were the tears she shed as she thought of him so far away:

O Lord, thou hear'st my daily moan,
and see'st my dropping tears,
my troubles all are thee before,
my longings and my fears.

Yet even as she wrote those words, she rebuked herself, for surely she had one with her who would never leave her desolate:

Though husband dear be from me gone,
whom I do love so well,
I have a more beloved One
whose comforts far excel.

Even at the times when she missed Simon's advice most and scarcely knew what to do, she still had a divine Counsellor at her side:

O stay my heart on thee, my God,
uphold my fainting soul,
and when I know not what to do,
I'll on thy mercies roll.

Despite her present circumstances Anne realized that this was an opportunity to make good those aspirations she had expressed on her recent recovery from illness — intentions to live 'a humble, faithful life' and walk more closely with her God. It is interesting to note that the poetry of this last period of Anne Bradstreet's life takes on a new and meeker tone. Gone for ever is the exalted phraseology, the classical rhetoric of her earlier work, and in its place has come a fresh devotion to Jesus Christ — a note often missing before:

O shine upon me, blessed Lord,
e'en for my Saviour's sake;
in thee alone is more than all
and there content I'll take.

With only her daughter Mercy, now fifteen, and nine-year-old John still at home, Anne had more leisure to meditate, more time to pray, more opportunities to wander in the woods near her home and to observe the wonders of the natural world. And always the beauties of God's handiwork proved a shortcut to thoughts of the Creator himself. As she saw the sunlight filtering through the trees, and thought of the dependence of the whole creation on the rays of the sun, she addressed her words to it:

Art thou so full of glory that no eye
hath strength thy shining rays once to behold? ...
How full of glory then must thy Creator be,
who gave this bright light lustre unto thee?
Adored, admired for ever, be that majesty.

Considered by some to be among her best, this poem, entitled 'Contemplations', has an unusual construction, each stanza consisting of seven lines. Not only does Anne ponder the grandeur of the creation and then worship the Creator, but she also grieves over the sad blight that now rests on all that she sees around her because of the fall of Adam and Eve in the Garden of Eden, with its resulting scar on humanity:

Man at the best a creature frail and vain,
in knowledge ignorant, in strength but weak,
subject to sorrows, losses, sickness, pain,
each storm his state, his mind, his body break;
from some of these he never finds cessation,
but day and night, within, without, vexation:
troubles from foes, from friends, from dearest, near'st
    relation.

But despite all that he suffers, Anne observes:

And yet this sinful creature, frail and vain,
this lump of wretchedness, of sin and sorrow,

this weather-beaten vessel wracked with pain,
joys not in hope of an eternal morrow,
nor all his losses, crosses, and vexation,
in weight, in frequency and long duration,
can make him deeply groan for that divine translation.

It would seem that her own thoughts were turning more and more to 'an eternal morrow'. Perhaps she had some premonition that she might not have much longer to live. Yet she was only just fifty, whereas her father had lived until he was seventy-seven. It would seem that Simon had written to her describing all the pomp and grandeur of the coronation he had witnessed. And yet, thought Anne sadly, as she contemplated the scene he described, time will eat away at all earthly magnificence, and bring it to nothing. Only the eternal treasures of the heavenly realm will endure. And with these observations, this time with eight lines, she ends this poem:

O Time, the fatal wrack [destroyer] of mortal things,
that draws oblivion's curtain over kings;
their sumptuous monuments, men know them not,
their names without a record are forgot,
their parts, their ports, their pomp's all laid in th' dust,
nor wit, nor gold, nor buildings 'scape time's rust;
but he whose name is graved in the white stone
shall last and shine when all of these are gone.

While Anne was musing on the uncertainties of life, Simon Bradstreet and his fellow negotiators were dealing with the uncertainties of procuring a favourable renewal of the Massachusetts Bay Colony charter from the new king. Changeable and lacking in seriousness, Charles II had to be handled with care. Eventually he did indeed grant a renewal of the charter, but the conditions on which he did so were prejudicial to the colonists' ideals and practices. First, the franchise had to be extended, allowing the vote to all males — non-church members as well as those who were in communion with the church. Secondly, the liturgical worship of the *Book of Common Prayer* must be observed in the churches. Nor was this the prayer book in use during the reign of Elizabeth I; rather it was the revised prayer book of 1662, to which all ministers in the homeland were obliged to give 'unfeigned assent and consent', or else risk losing both pulpit and livelihood.

While being well aware that both these conditions would be highly unacceptable to the General Court back in Massachusetts, Simon evidently decided that he had no alternative but to return home with such agreements as he had obtained. Perhaps the distance between England and her colony and the indifference of Charles to many matters of state might prevent any unwanted interference from the English court in New England affairs.

We can well imagine with what jubilation Anne greeted Simon's homecoming on 3 September 1662. He had been away for eighteen long months and, as was her custom, she sat down and wrote a celebratory poem to express her joy and thankfulness to God:

> *What shall I render to thy name*
> *or how thy praises speak,*
> *my thanks how shall I testify?*
> *O Lord, thou know'st I'm weak.*
>
> *What did I ask for but thou gav'st?*
> *What could I more desire?*

But thankfulness even all my days
I humbly this require.

Two further joys awaited Anne and Simon. Their eldest
son, Samuel, now aged twenty-eight, announced his
engagement to twenty-one-year-old Mercy Tyng, a young
woman with whom he was deeply in love. Perhaps he had
awaited his father's return before making the engagement
public. Naturally his mother's happiness was heartfelt, for
this son had a unique place in her affections and he had
remained single long enough. His younger sisters had
already married and were bringing up families, while she
herself had married when she was only sixteen. Having
completed his medical studies, Samuel planned to settle in
Boston and establish a practice there.

Soon after this Anne learnt that her own sister Mercy,
with her husband John Woodbridge and their family,
would be returning home to New England. Sixteen years
had elapsed since John had sailed off with Anne's manuscript tucked in his luggage; thirteen years had passed
since the publication of *The Tenth Muse*. Still a popular title,
the book was selling briskly, and John no longer need fear
Anne's disapproving looks over his actions. His decision to
return in 1663 was probably due to the ever-increasing
levels of persecution being levelled at Dissenters and
Nonconformists in England. Two thousand principled and
godly men had been evicted from their livings the previous
year because they were unable to agree to the terms of the
Act of Uniformity, which demanded total compliance with
every detail of the new *Book of Common Prayer*. The prisons
were fast filling up with men of conscience, and John

Woodbridge decided that it was best to put the Atlantic between himself and that merciless regime.

Meanwhile, Massachusetts itself was altering. The first leaders had died and, with the second and third generation growing into positions of influence, the standards were gradually changing. Some of the children and many of the grandchildren of the early settlers lacked the spiritual convictions of their fathers. Material concerns were taking precedence in the thinking of young Americans. As a result church membership was declining as the older generation died, with some churches struggling to keep their doors open. Under pressure to accommodate to this situation, the churches were beginning to accept upright but unregenerate men and women into a form of associate church member-ship known as the Halfway Covenant. Introduced in 1662, this arrangement allowed parents who had been baptized in infancy, although not themselves professing Christians, to have their own children baptized and to enjoy some of the privileges of church membership. Such a compromise would in turn result in a steady loss of evangelical fervour.

In the 1630s deviants from the 'Massachusetts way' such as Anne Hutchinson and Roger Williams had been hastily expelled from the colony in the interests of uniformity of religious views. But now, with the ever-increasing number of immigrants pouring into the colonies, such standards could no longer be maintained. The doors were being forced open by the arrival of Quakers, Baptists, and even Roman Catholics, all of whom were facing severe re-pressions under Charles II's government. John Endecott was once again in the governor's chair in Massachusetts and he, together with the court, feared that the ideals which the colony had striven to uphold over the years were being swiftly eroded. Persecution against the more extreme and disruptive Quakers was swift and harsh, even resulting in a number of public hangings in Boston. But still they came, men and women of many different religious persuasions or of none; throughout the 1660s and beyond they were settling in different enclaves as New England steadily developed.

Paul Johnson, writing on this period of early American history, comments that with a 'weakened church authority the social atmosphere became more secular and mercantile, and the Puritan merged into the Yankee'.[1] Now the artisan and trader began to take precedence over the Puritan and his spiritual aspirations — the materialist over men like Thomas Dudley and John Winthrop. The desire to prosper became steadily more dominant. But, as Anne Bradstreet wisely notes, the final end of those who live only for pleasure and advancement is bound to be disillusionment:

Fond fool, he takes this earth ev'n for heav'n's bower.
But sad affliction comes and makes him see
here's neither honour, wealth nor safety:
only above is found all with security.

14.
A house on high

Anne Bradstreet was delighted when Mercy, her eldest son Samuel's wife, announced that she was expecting her first child early in the summer of 1663. As we have seen, the bond between Anne and her son Samuel was close. His birth had been the answer to her many prayers, dispelling the fear that she might remain childless. That love for Samuel was now warmly extended to her new daughter-in-law, and so when Samuel arranged for his young wife to spend the last months of her pregnancy in Anne's care, she welcomed Mercy warmly. Little Elizabeth was safely born in Andover during February 1664 and the whole family was full of thankfulness.

Like Anne herself, Mercy was far from strong, so Samuel was glad for his wife to stay on in Andover under his mother's watchful eye. He himself was facing considerable pressure building up his medical practice in Boston, but whenever he could he visited Andover, with bonds of affection between the two families growing ever closer. The presence of a child in the home once more brought

Anne much pleasure, especially as she watched the baby's development. But she always knew that those delights could be cut off at any time, for she felt increasingly sure that her own days were drawing to a close. So certain was she of this that she sat down and composed a short account of her life for her children to act as a memorial when she had gone.[1] Unlike our own society, Anne was not inhibited about speaking of her forthcoming death; even so, she did not wish her family to read her words before she died:

> *This book by any yet unread,*
> *I leave for you when I am dead,*
> *that being gone, here you may find*
> *what was your living mother's mind.*
> *Make use of what I leave in love,*
> *and God shall bless you from above.*

The account, probably written in 1664, forms the basis of most of what we know of Anne Bradstreet's life apart from what may be gleaned from her poetry. She told of her childhood endeavours to please God, of her serious illness with smallpox, of her assurance of God's forgiveness, of her marriage to Simon and the dismay she felt at her dismal circumstances in the early days after her arrival in the New World. Her dread of childlessness and urgent prayers and tears before she became pregnant with her first child are all recorded here. She expresses her deep concern for her family's spiritual welfare, telling them that 'as I have brought you into the world, and with great pains, weakness, cares and fears brought you to this [time], I now travail in birth again ... till Christ be formed in you'.

Anne then told her family of the spiritual struggles she had experienced, of her temptations, doubts and battles.

She realized that she had needed God's chastening hand many times over. Above all, she had longed to know more of the presence of God with her soul:

> When I have been in sickness and pain, I have thought that if the Lord would but lift up the light of his countenance upon me, although he ground me to powder, it would be but light to me.

The answers to her prayers had given her that added measure of consolation that had balanced out her afflictions.

Surprisingly, in this account of her life Anne makes no mention of her poetry, nor of the extraordinary success of her book *The Tenth Muse*. She had learnt by many hard lessons to count her achievements as 'loss for Christ's sake'.

Those high hopes which she, like others, had entertained that Massachusetts would be a truly Christian state had been gradually eroded, and even more so in recent years. In case her children lost sight of those early ideals of the founders, Anne mentions with deep concern the present state of things. In her view the floodgates had been opened and 'the world has been filled with blasphemy and sectaries' — a reference to the excesses of the Quakers and others. But in her perplexity she recalled that Christ himself had spoken of days when 'even the elect' might be deceived if that were possible.

For herself, she concluded her 'memoirs' by reaffirming the solid foundation of her faith, Jesus Christ. Though acutely aware of her own frailty, she could say confidently:

> Upon this rock Christ Jesus will I build my faith, and if I perish, I perish, but I know all the powers of hell

*shall never prevail against it. I know whom I have
trusted, and whom I have believed and that he is able to
keep that I have committed to his charge.*

A noble and moving testimony, it was indeed a memorial to be treasured by her family, and not by them alone,
but by all who would read her words in future years.
Anne had a further memorial to bequeath to the family
she anticipated leaving shortly, this time dedicated to her
second son, Simon, now twenty-four years of age and
beginning in the ministry. Dated 20 March 1664, it took the
form of a fascinating selection of meditations — seventy-
seven in all — covering a wide variety of subjects which
she had been gathering over the years. From short prov-
erbs such as, 'Downy beds make drowsy persons, but hard
lodgings keep the eyes open,' with its corollary that adversity often benefits the believer, to wise observations on
childcare and cooking, Anne's reflections demonstrate an
unusual strength of mind. Most take the form of a parable
with its spiritual counterpart. Realizing how easily one
apparently small sin can lead onwards to a serious moral
collapse, Anne sagely comments:

> *That town which thousands of enemies without have
> not been able to take has been delivered up by one
> traitor within; and that man which all the temptations of
> Satan without could not hurt has been foiled by one lust
> within.*

Anne's meditations often make reference to the short-
ness and uncertainty of life. Man, she points out, is only a
tenant of his earthly house, his body; God, the 'great
Landlord', is the one who sets the bounds of each person's

The opening page of the letter, in Anne's own handwriting, which accompanied her 'meditations'

The concluding section of the letter shown on the previous page

life. And until God's time has come to conclude that tenancy, 'no dangers, no sickness, no pains nor troubles shall put an end to our days'. Yet the uncertainty of life should make each 'sure of an everlasting habitation that fades not away'.

How little did Anne realize, as she penned those words, their relevance to her own and her family's experiences so soon to come! She herself, despite her premonitions, still had longer to live than she had thought but, sadly, eighteen-month-old baby Elizabeth died in August 1665.

Whether the child had contracted one of those fevers that so frequently swept through the communities, or had even fallen prey to the dreaded smallpox, we do not know. Anne was devastated, as were Elizabeth's parents, Mercy and Samuel. Perhaps, Anne thought ruefully, she had loved the baby too much. Although she herself had not lost any of her eight children, this was in fact rare with the high infant mortality rate in the colonies. Anne's attitude to this bereavement, expressed in the lines she wrote, forms a marked contrast to views current in our own culture over such tragedies:

> *Farewell, dear babe, my heart's too much content,*
> *farewell, sweet babe, the pleasure of mine eye,*
> *farewell, fair flower that for a space was lent,*
> *then ta'en away unto eternity.*
> *Blest babe, why should I once bewail thy fate,*
> *or sigh thy days so soon were terminate,*
> *since thou art settled in an everlasting state?*

For Mercy herself, the death of her first child would have been particularly distressing, and may well have filled her with foreboding, for she was pregnant again. Would she lose this child as well? She remained in Andover living with her parents-in-law, and the whole community was cheered when a second daughter arrived safely five months after the loss of Elizabeth. Mercy and Samuel called their child Anne, and we may well imagine the delight this gave to Mercy's mother-in-law, a clear tribute to her devotion and care.

Meanwhile, Anne's own trials accelerated during these last years of her life, but few were as unexpected as an event of fearsome proportions which took place in July

1666. The family had all settled for the night when Anne was awoken suddenly by the sound of a 'thundering' and other unfamiliar noises. Alarmed, she sprang up, only to be greeted by 'piteous shrieks of dreadful voice'. 'Fire! Fire!' someone was yelling over and over again. Jumping out of bed, Anne's worst fears were confirmed: a sheet of flame and heat was licking up at the window. Colonial houses, made entirely from sawn planks of wood, were seriously vulnerable to threats of fire, and the large central kitchen fire, often throwing out sparks or even half burnt logs onto the hearth, constituted an ever-present danger. It seems that in this case one of the maids had dropped a candle on the floor and it had swiftly caught a curtain or cover, the flames spreading before the hapless girl could put out the blaze.

Part of the kitchen in a typical home of the period
Reproduced by courtesy of Kristina Stevick, History Alive! / Gordon
College Institute for Public History, MS.

Whether Anne's husband Simon was home at the time we are not told, but her first thought would clearly have been for Mercy and nine-month-old baby Anne. Having secured their safety, and accounted for every member of the household, she rushed outside, probably clad only in her nightwear. Together they could do nothing but watch in helpless disbelief as the whole home was destroyed in an inferno of heat.

In her great need Anne cried out to her God to:

> ... *strengthen me in my distress*
> *and not to leave me succourless.*

Able to bear no more, she found she could no longer watch as her personal possessions and everything she had called 'home' was destroyed. But with Job, who lost all he had in dire circumstances, she could say, 'I blest his name that gave and took.' At the death of baby Elizabeth she had owned that her God was the true possessor of all, and now, even at this moment of dark despair, she could bow in heart and say:

> *It was his own, it was not mine,*
> *far be it that I should repine.*

We can only marvel at such a noble reaction to her loss. But Anne was also human and felt the catastrophe deeply. In such a tight-knit community, undoubtedly neighbours and friends took the family in and supplied their immediate needs, but as she looked at the charred ruins of her home on the next day and the many days that followed, she grieved for the loss of her all. Their considerable library, which Anne had valued, had gone. She could

pinpoint the spot where her bed had been, where her
favourite chair had once stood, where a trunk, perhaps
containing her clothes, had formerly been placed — now
nothing but ashes remained. In one corner she once had a
wooden chest and in it 'there lay that store I counted best'.
We wonder what was in that chest; perhaps it contained
some treasured memorabilia, or it may even have held
manuscripts of unpublished poems. It appears that Anne
had not written any major verse during the last ten years of
her life, yet it is possible that some of her work was lost in
the fire. She hints as much in the final lines of her unfinished quaternion called 'The Four Monarchies'. There we
learn that she had been trying without success to conclude
her work on the Roman dynasty:

> But 'fore I could accomplish my desire,
> my papers fell a prey to th' raging fire.
> And thus my pains (with better things) I lost,
> which none have cause to wail, nor I to boast.

Not only did she grieve for the loss of her possessions;
her home had stood for far more than these: it represented
many incidents that had taken place within those four walls
during the past twenty years of her life. Three of her children had been born there; many a guest had sat round her
table, chatting and enjoying her hospitality. Her son Samuel
and daughter-in-law Mercy had probably been married
there. Addressing the desolate ruins, she writes sadly:

> Under thy roof no guest shall sit,
> nor at thy table eat a bit.
> No pleasant tale shall e'er be told,
> nor things recounted done of old.

No candle e'er shall shine in thee,
nor bridegroom's voice e'er heard shall be.
In silence ever shalt thou lie,
Adieu, Adieu, all's vanity.

At this point in her account Anne rebukes herself sharply. God had surely been teaching her again a lifelong lesson that nothing on this earth is truly permanent. Indignantly she asks herself:

Didst fix thy hope on mould'ring dust,
The arm of flesh didst make thy trust?

She of all people should know that life for the believer is a pilgrimage to a better world. Had she not left her luxurious home in England to settle in the wilderness of the New World with that very principle in mind? Surely she must remain a pilgrim right to the end:

Thou hast an house on high erect,
framed by that mighty Architect
with glory richly furnishèd,
stands permanent though this be fled.

The purchase price of that home above was costly, yet Christ had paid the whole for her. In that land, she asserts, 'there's wealth enough, I need no more'.

We are glad to know that Simon soon set his sawmill going, losing no time in building and furnishing a new earthly home for Anne and his family — a much more permanent edifice that still stands today in North Andover.

15.
Seeking a better country

As Anne Bradstreet gazed at the blackened ruins of her home, how little could she have guessed that this disaster for her family would soon be dwarfed by that far greater conflagration which was to destroy much of London a mere six weeks later! When Thomas Farynor, Charles II's baker, forgot to shut down his oven on the night of Sunday, 2 September 1666, a fire was ignited that would blaze for five days, destroying eighty-seven of London's old churches. More than thirteen thousand homes were consumed in the flames, with one and a half square miles of the sprawling capital reduced to ashes. Following so soon after her own experience, Anne could feel the horror of such a tragedy, yet it must have reinforced the lifelong lesson she was gradually learning — that the best this world can offer is only transitory.

With her new home built, Anne quickly moved in, together with Samuel's wife Mercy and their young daughter, also named Anne. By this time Anne's own girls were all married, and were scattered in different New England

The new house built on the site of the one destroyed by fire

townships; only the two younger boys remained at home. Dudley, now eighteen, was helping his father Simon in overseeing the farm and the sawmill business, while John, still only fourteen, was continuing his education. Anne herself was by now fifty-four years of age, and the long periods of illness, coupled with her eight pregnancies, had permanently undermined her health. Increasing frailty, compounded by frequent bouts of fever, left her looking ever more expectantly to a better country — the true home of the believer — that she had so long anticipated. Somehow the loss of her previous home had snapped her ties with material things, as she had written:

> The world no longer let me love,
> my hope and treasure lies above.

In one of the meditations she had presented to her son
Simon, she had expressed the same thought under the
image of a journey:

> *He that is to sail into a far country, although the ship,*
> *cabin and provision be all convenient and comfortable*
> *for him, yet he has no desire to make that his place of*
> *residence, but longs to put in at that port where his*
> *business lies. A Christian is sailing through this world*
> *unto his heavenly country and here he has many con-*
> *veniences and comforts, but he must beware of desiring*
> *to make this the place of his abode... We must, there-*
> *fore, be here as strangers and pilgrims, that we may*
> *plainly declare that we seek a city above...*

In late 1667, some fifteen months after the fire, Mercy and
her husband Samuel were gladdened by the arrival of
another healthy baby daughter, whom they called Mercy.
Perhaps the presence in the house of Anne's small grandchildren was one of those comforts to which she had al-
luded in her meditation quoted above and one which must
have charmed her the most during these years. But it was
for her namesake, little Anne, now turned two years of age,
that she felt a particular tenderness. The child's cheerful
chatter brightened her days and kept her fully occupied,
while Mercy's uncertain health and the new baby's needs
called for Anne's constant care. In the intervals between
watching over the children she was working steadily on her
poems as she tried to complete an improved version for a
possible second edition of *The Tenth Muse*, now in demand.
Her dismay at the early publication of her unrevised work
had given way to a determination to rewrite some poems
and correct others until she was satisfied with the result.

And then in June 1669 the family once more experienced an unexpected grief. Anne's granddaughter Anne, now just over three and a half, suddenly sickened and died. Anne's distress is palpable as she wrote sadly:

> *With troubled heart and trembling hand I write,*
> *the heavens have changed to sorrow my delight.*

Yet even as she expressed such a thought, she had to add:

> *How oft with disappointment have I met,*
> *when I on fading things my hopes have set.*

Anne was no stoic, nor did she feel that she must bottle up her anguish as she asks herself:

> *Was ever stable joy yet found below,*
> *or perfect bliss without mixture of woe?*

She recognized that this treasured little girl was 'but as a withering flower, that's here today, perhaps gone in an hour'. She chided herself mercilessly for the depth of her affection:

> *More fool then I to look on what was lent*
> *as if my own, when thus impermanent.*

Such a loss sharpened her own longings for heaven and, using the words of King David when his infant died, she wrote:

> *Farewell, dear child, thou ne'er shall come to me,*
> *but yet a while and I shall go to thee.*

Above all, she had one strong consolation:

Meantime my throbbing heart's cheered up with this:
thou with my Saviour art in endless bliss.

The child's death must have been particularly hard for her mother to bear as she was pregnant once more. Mercy's first child, Elizabeth, had died at eighteen months and now her second had gone, leaving her with only one infant daughter, Mercy. Undoubtedly affected by the circumstances, she gave premature birth soon afterwards to her first son. But this child, whom she named Simon after her father-in-law, was not strong enough to contend with life for long, and died at just a month old. As Anne put it:

No sooner came, but gone, and fall'n asleep,
acquaintance short, yet parting caused us weep.

She added the comment:

... three flowers, two scarcely blown, the last i' the bud,
cropped by th' Almighty's hand — yet is he good.
With dreadful awe before him let's be mute,
such was his will, but why, let's not dispute.

A day would come, Anne stated in hopeful confidence, when Christ himself would 'make up our losses' and they would 'smile again after our bitter crosses'. Then with a word to the child so recently taken, Anne ended:

Go, pretty babe, go rest with sisters twain,
among the blest in endless joys remain.

If Anne and the children's mother, Mercy, felt the loss of these three infants in quick succession so acutely, we can well imagine the effect on their father, Samuel, the eldest son of Anne and Simon. Seeking to establish his medical practice in Boston, and in consequence seeing little of his fragile wife Mercy, he was wrestling with a big decision. As his parents had once emigrated from England, seeking a land where they could live and worship in peace, so Samuel's mind was turning ever more towards some escape route from the country of his own birth, which he could now only see in a gloomy light. Mercy needed a different climate in order to recover strength. So Samuel ultimately set his heart on the long journey to Jamaica, where the warmth and constancy of temperature might be of benefit to her.

Although he knew that his mother would not find such a decision easy to accept, for at her age she would be unlikely to see either Samuel or Mercy ever again, he went ahead with his plans. The situation became yet more urgent when Mercy discovered that she was pregnant once more. If Samuel did not act quickly the life of this expected child could also be short. With little time to lose he decided to go to Jamaica ahead of his wife, establish a home for her and for their children, and then bring the family to Jamaica. With this purpose in mind he set sail shortly before the baby was due.

Anne appears to have kept silent about these decisions. She may well have feared the worst, for Mercy's health was failing and she missed her husband's support at such a time. On 3 September 1670, shortly after Samuel had set out for Jamaica, Mercy once again gave premature birth, this time to another daughter. Perhaps with more fear than hope, she named her infant Anne once more — maybe this child would live and be a reminder to her of the cheerful toddler she had lost the previous year. But following her confinement Mercy's condition deteriorated rapidly and, with Samuel far away, his wife — still only twenty-eight years of age — died three days after the child's birth. Nor could the new little Anne survive long without her mother, and she too died within the week.

With Samuel on his way to Jamaica and only little Mercy left of the five children Mercy had borne to him, Anne wrote sadly to her son breaking the news of his loss and at the same time dedicating her lines to Mercy as a tribute to this dearly-loved daughter-in-law:

> *I saw the branches lopped, the tree now fall,*
> *I stood so nigh, it crushed me down withal.*
> *My bruisèd heart lies sobbing at the root,*
> *that thou, dear son, hath lost both tree and fruit.*
> *Thou, then on seas sailing to foreign coast,*
> *wast ignorant what riches thou hadst lost.*

How would Samuel cope with such grief? His mother could express her deep sympathy:

> *Oh, how I sympathize with thy sad heart*
> *and in thy griefs still bear a second part;*
> *I lost a daughter dear, but thou a wife*
> *who loved thee more (it seemed) than her own life.*
> *Thou being gone, she longer could not be,*
> *because her soul she'd sent along with thee.*

She reminded Samuel too of the one child he had still remaining:

> *She one hath left, a joy to thee and me,*
> *the heavens vouchsafe she may so ever be.*

But Anne was not one to flounder in her sorrows. She had learnt long ago where to look in such times. So now she urges her son to find that same source of consolation:

Cheer up, dear son, thy fainting bleeding heart,
in him alone that caused all this smart.
What though thy strokes full sad and grievous be,
he knows it is the best for thee and me.

Despite her courageous bearing, Mercy's death seemed to hasten Anne's own. She was now fifty-eight, considered elderly in days when life expectancy was far lower than today. So now her thoughts were turning ever more frequently towards the end of her pilgrimage — a concept of life that had never been far from her mind:

A pilgrim I, on earth perplexed
with sins, with cares, with sorrows vexed,
by age and pains brought to decay,
and my clay house mould'ring away.
Oh, how I long to be at rest,
and soar on high among the blest!

Tears and loss had filled these last years of Anne Bradstreet's life, but she looked on in hope for that day when:

Mine eyes no more shall ever weep,
no fainting fits shall me assail,
nor grinding pains my body frail;
with cares and fears ne'er cumbered be
nor losses know, nor sorrows see.

Recalling words of Scripture, she could write:

And when a few years shall be gone,
this mortal shall be clothed upon ...
in weakness and dishonour sown,
in power 'tis raised by Christ alone.

With willing heart Anne could now pray:

Lord, make me ready for that day,
then come, dear Bridegroom, come away.

And it was a prayer that God granted. Suffering from tuberculosis once more and with her body sadly 'wasted', as one son recorded, Anne Bradstreet died on 16 September 1672 with her husband Simon at her side. Just two years had elapsed since Mercy's death and Samuel's departure for Jamaica. She was missed sorely by her husband, who had perhaps taken more interest in his business concerns and in the politics of the colony than in his wife's needs. Simon, who would eventually occupy the governor's chair, did not remarry for four years — an unusually long time in that society, and possibly a tribute to their shared love.

Although no record of Anne's last words has been preserved for us, and even her grave has been obliterated by time, so that no one knows exactly where she was buried, her legacy lives on. As Cotton Mather, an early New England historian, rightly observes, Anne Bradstreet's poetry remains 'a monument for her memory beyond the stateliest marble'.[1] As America's first published poet — an astonishing achievement, particularly for a woman in the face of the prejudice of the times — her work is still studied and highly valued today and her life remembered.

In 1678, six years after her death, a second edition of Anne Bradstreet's poetry was published in Boston,[2] this time bearing the title *Several Poems* — a much more modest description than *The Tenth Muse,* and one that probably reflected Anne's own distaste for the somewhat grandiose title originally chosen by John Woodbridge. Included in this second edition were many of the more personal poems of Anne's later years — ones that bear eloquent testimony to the strength of her faith. The title page also announces boldly that the poems had been 'corrected by the author'. A further manuscript would later come to light and a complete portfolio of her work was published in 1857, while a number of editions of her poetry are still in print today.

Anne's work reveals a sharp wit, with occasional verbal banter, and extraordinary classical learning. It manifests a tender sensitivity and a love of beauty, relating all that she saw and experienced to God as the first cause of all things, together with a humble submission to his will, however perplexing it might seem at times.

On a wider canvas, and yet more crucially, Anne Bradstreet was among the first to lay down markers for the ethos and mindset of a new, young country — America. The strong spiritual convictions that shaped the nation's early laws, the aspirations of its Puritan founders and the biblical truths that underpinned its society can still find an echo in American life today. All these were given a human voice in the writings of Anne Bradstreet — mother of eight and secret poet. The publication of *The Tenth Muse* in 1650 impressed on English society that their colony, New England, was a separate culture, a fresh entity, with a mind and traditions of its own.

SEVERAL

POEMS

Compiled with great variety of Wit and
Learning, full of Delight;
Wherein especially is contained a compleat
Discourse, and Description of

The Four ⎨ ELEMENTS.
⎨ CONSTITUTIONS,
⎨ AGES of Man,
⎨ SEASONS of the Year.

Together with an exact Epitome of
the three first *Monarchyes*

Viz. The ⎨ *ASSYRIAN,*
⎨ *PERSIAN,*
⎨ *GRECIAN.*

And beginning of the Romane Common-wealth
to the end of their last King :

With diverse other pleasant & serious *Poems,*

By a Gentlewoman in *New-England.*

The second Edition, Corrected by the Author
and enlarged by an Addition of several other
Poems found amongst her Papers
after her Death.

Boston, Printed by *John Foster,* 1678.

Title-page of the second edition of Anne's poems

Despite having no record of their mother's last words, Anne's children received a bequest of greater value — a personal account of her life and also many wise observations expressed in the seventy-seven meditations dedicated to her son Simon. Here they would find guidelines for living in a way that was pleasing to God, and a declaration of those motives that had governed her own priorities. In one such reflection she points out that if God has given any special gifts to a person (as he undoubtedly had to Anne Bradstreet), those same gifts carry weighty responsibilities and must be diligently employed in his service:

> *Great receipts call for great returns; the more any man is trusted withal, the larger his accounts stand upon God's score. It therefore behoves every man so to improve his talents that when his great master shall call him to reckoning, he may receive his own with advantage.*

But, above all, Anne Bradstreet saw the path of a Christian through this world as a pilgrimage. At the age of eighteen she had exchanged old England for New, an event that stamped this perspective permanently on her thinking. Yet, like the patriarchs, she was always eagerly 'seeking a better country, that is a heavenly, whose builder and maker is God'. Her words, born out of the joys and trials of her life, still resonate in the experience and aspirations of Christian men and women today:

> *If I of heaven may have my fill,*
> *take thou the world and all that will.*

Appendix
Anne Bradstreet's biographical account left for her family

My dear children,

I, knowing by experience that the exhortations of parents take most effect when the speakers leave to speak, and those especially sink deepest which are spoke latest, and being ignorant whether on my deathbed I shall have opportunity to speak to any of you, much less to all, thought it the best, whilst I was able, to compose some short matters (for what else to call them I know not) and bequeath to you, that when I am no more with you, yet I may be daily in your remembrance (although that is the least in my aim in what I now do), but that you may gain some spiritual advantage by my experience. I have not studied in this you read to show my skill, but to declare the truth, not to set forth myself, but the glory of God. If I had minded the former, it had been perhaps better pleasing to you, but seeing the last is the best, let it be best pleasing to you.

The method I will observe shall be this: I will begin with God's dealing with me from my childhood to this day.

In my young years, about 6 or 7 as I take it, I began to make conscience of my ways, and what I knew was sinful, as lying, disobedience to parents, etc., I avoided it. If at any time I was overtaken with the like evils, it was as a great trouble, and I could not be at rest 'till by prayer I had confessed it unto God. I was also troubled at the neglect of private duties though too often tardy that way. I also found much comfort in reading the Scriptures, especially those places I thought most concerned my condition, and as I grew to have more understanding, so the more solace I took in them.

In a long fit of sickness which I had on my bed I often communed with my heart and made my supplication to the Most High who set me free from that affliction.

But as I grew up to be about 14 or 15, I found my heart more carnal, and sitting loose from God, vanity and the follies of youth take hold of me.

About 16, the Lord laid his hand sore upon me and smote me with the smallpox. When I was in my affliction, I besought the Lord and confessed my pride and vanity, and he was entreated of me and again restored me. But I rendered not to him according to the benefit received.

After a short time I changed my condition and was married, and came into this country, where I found a new world and new manners, at which my heart rose. But after I was convinced it was the way of God, I submitted to it and joined to the church at Boston.

After some time I fell into a lingering sickness like a consumption together with a lameness, which correction I saw the Lord sent to humble and try me and do me good, and it was not altogether ineffectual.

It pleased God to keep me a long time without a child, which was a great grief to me and cost me many prayers and tears before I obtained one, and after him gave me many more of whom I now take the care, that as I have brought you into the world, and with great pains, weakness, cares, and fears brought you to this, I now travail in birth again of you till Christ be formed in you.

Among all my experiences of God's gracious dealings with me, I have constantly observed this, that he hath never suffered me long to sit loose from him, but by one affliction or other hath made me look home, and search what was amiss; so usually thus it hath been with me that I have no sooner felt my heart out of order, but I have expected correction for it; which most commonly hath been upon my own person in sickness, weakness, pains, sometimes on my soul, in doubts and fears of God's displeasure and my sincerity towards him; sometimes he hath smote a child with a sickness, sometimes chastened by losses in estate, and these times (through his great mercy) have been the times of my greatest getting and advantage; yea, I have found them the times when the Lord hath manifested the most love to me. Then have I gone to searching and have said with David, 'Lord, search me and try me, see what ways of wickedness are in me, and lead me in the way everlasting,' and seldom or never but I have found either some sin I lay under which God would have reformed or some duty neglected which he would have performed, and by his help I have laid vows and bonds upon my soul to perform his righteous commands.

If at any time you are chastened of God, take it as thankfully and joyfully as in greatest mercies, for if ye be his, ye shall reap the greatest benefit by it. It hath been no small support to me in times of darkness when the Almighty hath hid his face from me that yet I have had abundance of sweetness and refreshment after affliction and more circumspection in my walking after I have been afflicted. I have been with God like an untoward child, that no longer than the rod has been on my back (or at least in sight) but I have been apt to forget him and myself, too. 'Before I was afflicted, I went astray, but now I keep thy statutes.'

I have had great experience of God's hearing my prayers and returning comfortable answers to me, either in granting the thing I prayed for, or else in satisfying my mind without it, and I have been confident it hath been from him, because I have found my heart through his goodness enlarged in thankfulness to him.

I have often been perplexed that I have not found that constant joy in my pilgrimage and refreshing which I supposed most of the servants of God have, although he hath not left me altogether without the witness of his Holy Spirit, who hath oft given me his word and set to his seal that it shall be well with me. I have sometimes tasted of that hidden manna that the world knows not, and have set up my Ebenezer and have resolved with myself that against such a promise, such tastes of sweetness, the gates of hell shall never prevail; yet have I many times sinkings and droopings, and not enjoyed that felicity that some-times I have done. But when I have been in darkness and seen no light, yet have I desired to stay myself upon the Lord, and when I have been in weakness and pain, I have thought if the Lord would but lift up the light of his coun-tenance upon me, although he ground me to powder, it would be but light to me; yea, oft have I thought were I in hell itself and could there find the love of God toward me, it would be a heaven. And could I have been in heaven without the love of God, it would have been a hell to me, for in truth it is the absence and presence of God that makes heaven or hell.

Many times hath Satan troubled me concerning the verity of the Scriptures, many times by atheism how I could know whether there was a God; I never saw any miracles to confirm me, and those which I read of, how did I know but they were feigned? That there is a God my reason would soon tell me by the wondrous works that I see, the vast frame of the heaven and the earth, the order of all things, night and day, summer and winter, spring and autumn, the daily providing for this great household upon the earth, the preserving and directing of all to its proper end. The consideration of these things would with amazement certainly resolve me that there is an Eternal Being. But how should I know he is such a God as I worship in Trinity, and such a Saviour as I rely upon? Though this hath thousands of times been suggested to me, yet God hath helped me over. I have argued thus with myself. That there is a God, I see. If ever this God hath revealed himself, it must be in his word, and this must be it or none. Have I not found that operation by it that no human invention can work upon the soul, hath not judgements befallen divers who have scorned and contemned it, hath it not been preserved through all ages maugre [i.e., in spite of] all the heathen tyrants and all of the enemies who have opposed it? Is there any story but that which shows the beginnings of times, and how the world came to be as we see? Do we not know the prophecies in it fulfilled which could not have been so long foretold by any but God himself?

When I have got over this block, then have I another put in my way, that admit this be the true God whom we worship, and that be his word, yet why may not the Popish religion be the right? They have the same God, the same Christ, the same word. They only interpret it one way, we another.

This hath sometimes stuck with me, and more it would, but the vain fooleries that are in their religion together with their lying miracles and cruel persecutions of the saints, which admit were they as they term them, yet not so to be dealt withal.

The consideration of these things and many the like would soon turn me to my own religion again.

But some new troubles I have had since the world has been filled with blasphemy and sectaries, and some who have been accounted sincere Christians have been carried away with them, that sometimes I have said, 'Is there faith upon the earth?' and I have not known what to think; but then I have remembered the words of Christ that so it must be, and if it were possible, the very elect should be deceived. 'Behold,' saith our Saviour, 'I have told you before.' That hath stayed my heart, and I can now say, 'Return, O my Soul, to thy rest, upon this rock Christ Jesus will I build my faith, and if I perish, I perish'; but I know all the powers of hell shall never prevail against it. I know whom I have trusted, and whom I have believed, and that he is able to keep that I have committed to his charge.

Now to the King, immortal, eternal and invisible, the only wise God, be honour, and glory for ever and ever, Amen.

This was written in much sickness and weakness, and is very weakly and imperfectly done, but if you can pick any benefit out of it, it is the mark which I aimed at.

Notes

Chapter 2 — The Great Migration
1. Earlier accounts suggest that this sermon was preached on board the *Arbella*, but more recently historian Francis Bremer has pointed out that if were so it would only have been heard by a small proportion of the emigrants (*John Winthrop, America's Forgotten Founding Father*, OUP, 2003). Most probably it was preached to all who were emigrating while they were waiting in Southampton.

Chapter 8 — The two dialogues
1. Anne had originally written, 'Farewell dear Mother, Parliament cause prevail,' but later diplomacy caused her to change the wording.

Chapter 9 — 'My rambling brat'
1. Romans 13:1-5.

Chapter 13 — Gathering clouds
1. Paul Johnson, *The History of the American People*, London: Weidenfeld & Nicolson, 1997, p.46.

Chapter 14 — A house on high
1. See the appendix.

Chapter 15 — Seeking a better country
1. Cotton Mather, *The Great Works of Christ in America*, reprinted Banner of Truth, 1979, vol. 1, p.135.
2. Thought to have been edited by a John Rogers, an early and ardent admirer of Anne's work, whose long eulogistic poem finds a place in current editions of her verse. Rogers married Anne's niece and later became president of Harvard College.

Suggestions for further reading

Anne Bradstreet's life and verse

Charlotte Gordon, *Mistress Bradstreet — the Untold Life of America's First Poet*, New York: Little, Brown and Company, 2005.

Heidi L Nichols, *Anne Bradstreet, A Guided Tour of the Life and Thought of a Puritan Poet*, New Jersey: P&R Publishing, 2006.

Elizabeth Wade White, *Anne Bradstreet, The Tenth Muse*, New York: 1971.

Jeannine Hensley, ed., *The Works of Anne Bradstreet*, Cambridge, Massachusetts: The Belknap Press of Harvard University Press, 1967.

Background reading

John Adair, *Founding Fathers. The Puritans in England and America*, London: J. M. Dent & Sons Ltd, 1982.

Edmund S. Morgan, *The Puritan Dilemma, The Story of John Winthrop*, Boston: Little, Brown and Company, 1958.

Francis J. Bremer, *The Puritan Experiment*, London: St James Press, 1976.

Paul Johnson, *The History of the American People*, London: Weidenfeld & Nicolson, 1997.

Cotton Mather, *The Great Works of Christ in America*, reprinted, Banner of Truth Trust, 1979.

Kelly Kapic and Randall Gleason (eds.), *The Devoted Life, an invitation to the Puritan classics*, Illinois: IVP, 2004.

Index

Aggawam — see Ipswich
Andover, 90, 91, 98, 103, 116, 128, 131, 139, 145
   Bradstreets' new house after the fire, 149, 150-51
antinomianism, 41
Arbella, the, 23, 26-8, 29

Book of Common Prayer, 135, 136
Boston, Lincolnshire, 13, 14, 32, 37, 121
   St Botolph's Church, 14, 15, 37, 120
Boston, Mass., 32, 38, 39, 41, 47, 70, 89, 121, 127, 136, 138, 139, 155, 159, 164
Bowtell, Stephen, 102-3, 104
Bradstreet, Anne,
   America's first published poet, 9-10, 158
   awareness of God's love in the midst of trials, 109-10, 114, 116, 117, 165
   begins to write poetry, 57
   birth, 12
   childhood, 12-17, 163-4

children, 45, 49, 64, 68, 69, 79, 92, 93-4, 95, 98, 108, 110, 132, 139, 148, 150-51, 161, 164-5
   care and prayers for, 121, 123-4, 140, 165
   concerns for in the event of her death, 93
   longing for, 35, 45, 140, 164
   poem describing them as a brood of nestlings, 119-25
'Contemplations', 133-4
death, 158
death of her father, 111
desires for heaven, 77, 110, 134, 151, 157-8, 161
devotion to Christ, 132
doubts and fears, 51-2, 110, 113-14, 140, 165, 167-8
'Dialogue between Old England and New, A', 81-7, 95, 106
early poems, 34, 35-6, 57-8, 60-66
education, 13, 16, 35, 95

Bradstreet, Anne (cont.),
    faith in God, 51, 52, 63, 73,
        106, 110, 115, 141-2, 159,
        168
    first edition of her poetry —
        see *The Tenth Muse*
    first impressions of the New
        World, 30, 140, 164
    'Flesh and the Spirit, The',
        75-8
    'Four Monarchies, The', 95,
        148
    four quaternions, the, 58,
        60-64, 65, 95
    grandchildren, 139-40, 144-5,
        152, 153-6
        poems marking deaths of,
            145, 147, 153-4
    house destroyed by fire,
        145-9
    illnesses, 72, 78-9, 109-10,
        113-17, 124, 127, 141, 151
        at nineteen, 34-5, 78, 164
        during childhood, 16-17,
            164
        final, 158
        smallpox, 18, 78, 140, 164
    joins church in Boston, 31,
        164
    lessons learnt from daily
        life, 70-71
    letter accompanying her
        'meditations', 143-4
    life at Ipswich, 53-5, 67-74

    loneliness in Simon's ab-
        sence, 55, 68, 69, 71, 73-4,
        75, 98, 114-15, 131-2
    loss of her mother, 88-9, 93,
        98
    love for husband, 18-19, 35,
        68-9, 73-4, 94
    marriage, 18, 20, 140, 164
    'meditations',   69-71,   75,
        142-4, 161
    'memoir',   78,   140-42,   161,
        163-8
    move to Andover, 90, 92, 95
    move to Ipswich, 47-9
    new house built after fire,
        149, 150-51
    poem on the death of her
        daughter-in-law, 156-7
    poem to celebrate Simon's
        homecoming, 135-6
    poetry (see also *Several
        Poems, The Tenth Muse* and
        entries relating to indi-
        vidual poems), 9-10, 19,
        34, 36, 41, 46, 57-8, 60-66,
        68-9, 71-8, 81-7, 89, 92-6,
        98-108, 111-29, 131-6, 138,
        140, 145, 147-9, 151, 152-4,
        156-61
    praise for son's safe return
        from England, 128-9
    prayers, 17, 49, 72-3, 110, 117
        answered, 17, 72, 99, 114,
            128, 129, 135, 141, 166

for a child, 35, 45, 119, 139, 140, 164

for forgiveness, 14, 18, 140

for husband when he goes to England, 126-7

for son when he sails to England, 119

reliance on God, 70, 71-2, 78, 109, 115, 117, 127, 132, 166

response to the execution of Charles I, 103-4

response to publication of *The Tenth Muse*, 106-8, 152

second edition of poems — see *Several Poems*

sense of indebtedness and accountability to God, 109

Several Poems, 152, 159, 160

struggles against temptations (see also 'doubts and fears'), 75-8, 115, 140, 167

torn loyalties over the Civil War in England, 81, 92

teenage years, 17-18, 164

Tenth Muse, The, 9, 100-108, 109, 116, 136, 141, 152, 159

thankfulness for restored health, 114, 118, 127

tribute to her father, 40-41, 111-13

urge to write poetry, 55-6

'Vanity of all Worldly Things, The', 92, 94

view of life as a pilgrimage, 73, 94, 149, 152, 157, 161

voyage to New England, 23, 25-8

Bradstreet, Anne (granddaughter), 145, 147, 150, 152, 153-4, 155

Bradstreet, Anne (granddaughter who died shortly after birth), 155-6

Bradstreet, Dorothy, 49, 64, 79, 121

Bradstreet, Dudley, 98, 110, 122, 151

Bradstreet, Elizabeth, 139, 144-5, 147, 154

Bradstreet, Hannah, 79, 122

Bradstreet, John, 108, 110, 116, 123, 132, 151

Bradstreet, Mercy (daughter), 94, 98, 123, 132

Bradstreet, Mercy (daughter-in-law), 136, 139, 145, 147, 148, 150, 152, 154, 155-7, 158

Bradstreet, Mercy (granddaughter), 152, 154, 156

Bradstreet, Samuel, 45, 47, 64, 79, 98, 136, 139, 145, 148, 152, 154-8, 164

absence in England, 118-19, 121, 127-9

loss of wife and baby, 155-7

Bradstreet, Sarah, 55, 64, 79, 121-2

Bradstreet Simon (grandson), 154

Bradstreet, Simon (husband), 17, 18-19, 20, 32, 33, 44, 45, 47, 49, 53, 64, 67-9, 90, 91-2, 93, 95, 112, 122, 136, 147, 149, 151, 158
  absences on business, 55, 67-9, 71, 73-4, 75, 89, 98, 114-15
  sent to England on behalf of colony, 126-7, 130-32, 134-5

Bradstreet, Simon (son), 64, 79, 122, 142, 143, 152

Cambridge — see New Towne

Charles I, King, 20, 21, 22, 50, 79-81, 85, 92, 94, 97-8, 99, 101, 130
  execution, 103

Charles II, King, 125, 130, 131, 134, 135, 137

Charlestown, 30, 32, 33, 90

Civil War, the English, 63, 79, 88, 92, 98, 103

Cotton, John, 14, 32, 37, 38, 39, 40, 41, 42, 126

Cotton, Seaborn, 121

Cromwell, Oliver, 44, 125

Cromwell, Richard,125

Denison, Captain, 47

du Bartas, Guillaume, 35-6, 57, 65, 100

Dudley, Anne — see Bradstreet, Anne

Dudley, Dorothy, 12, 14-15, 25, 70, 88-9, 111

Dudley, Mary, 47

Dudley, Mercy (Mercy Woodbridge), 12, 26, 47, 88, 90, 94, 98, 108, 136

Dudley, Patience, 12, 26, 47, 88, 91

Dudley, Samuel, 12, 47

Dudley, Sarah, 12, 26, 47, 88, 89

Dudley, Thomas, 12, 13, 16, 17, 21, 30, 32, 33, 38, 40-41, 43, 44, 47, 49, 57-8, 64-5, 67, 70, 89-90, 98, 111-13, 126, 134, 138
  encouragement of Anne, 64, 66, 111
  governor of the colony, 39, 42, 111

Elizabeth, dowager Countess of Lincoln, 13, 21

Endecott, John, 22, 29, 137

Great Fire of London, the, 150

Great Migration, the, 9, 23-4

Halfway Covenant, the, 137

Harvard, John, 91

Harvard College, 90-91, 112, 122

Hooker, Thomas, 21

Hopkins, Anne, 55-6
Hubbard, Richard, 121
Hutchinson, Anne, 36, 37-43, 47, 49, 52, 55, 56, 57, 64, 87, 137

intolerance of dissent,
    among the colonists, 38, 40, 42, 101
    in the English state church, 11-12, 16, 21, 136
Ipswich (Aggawam), 47, 48, 49, 50, 53, 57, 68, 70, 73, 79, 88, 89, 90, 91, 95, 122

James I, King, 11-12, 16, 20
Johnson, Lady Arbella, 21, 22, 23, 25, 31
Johnson, Isaac, 21, 22, 31
Johnson, Paul, 138

Laud, William, 21, 38, 50, 80
Lincoln, Earl of (Theophilus), 12, 13, 14, 17, 20

Massachusetts Bay, 2, 24, 42, 45
    Colony, 22, 36, 40, 81, 125
        changes in by 1660s, 137-8, 141
        charter, 22, 39, 81, 130, 134-5
        governors, 25, 38-9, 40, 42, 55, 111, 137, 158
    Company, 21-2

General Court, 39, 42, 49, 51, 92, 135, 137
    hit by devastating storm, 46-7
Mather, Cotton, 158
Mayflower, the — see Pilgrim Fathers

New Towne (Cambridge), 33, 45, 47, 53, 90
Northampton, Earl of, 12

Parker, Thomas, 50
Pilgrim Fathers, the, 16, 21, 33
    prejudice against women writers, 36, 55-6, 64, 65-6, 81, 100, 158
Puritans, 9, 11, 12, 13, 14, 17, 20, 21, 22, 24, 83, 86, 94, 103, 122, 138, 159

Quakers, 137, 138, 141

Rhode Island, 44
Roxbury, 70, 89

Salem, 29, 30, 43
Sempringham, 12, 14, 17, 21
Separatists, 16, 21, 22, 33
smallpox, 30, 145
    Anne suffers from, 18, 78, 140
state, control over church and conscience, 43-4, 51

suffering, God's purposes in, 69, 78, 116, 118, 142, 165-6

Theophilus — see Lincoln, Earl of
Tyng, Mercy — see Bradstreet, Mercy (daughter-in-law)

Uniformity, Act of, 136

Vane, Henry, 41-2

Ward, Nathaniel, 48, 49-52, 56-7, 66, 90, 94-5, 97, 101-2, 103, 126
  Body of Liberties, 50
  Simple Cobbler of Aggawam, 56-7, 101-2, 103

support for the publication of Anne's poetry, 100
Wheelwright, John, 40
Williams, Roger, 21, 43-4, 47, 111, 137
Wilson, John, 32, 38, 39-40
Winthrop, John, 21, 24-5, 30, 31, 32, 38, 39, 40, 42, 43, 44, 47, 50, 55, 111, 126, 138
  'City on a hill' sermon, 24, 25
  journal, 27-8
Woodbridge, John, 90, 91, 94, 95, 96, 97, 98, 103, 108, 136-7
  arranges publication of Anne's poems, 99-100, 102, 104-6, 159
Woodbridge, Mercy — see Dudley, Mercy
worship, freedom of, 24, 25, 44